Yemane Gidey

Assessment of Promotional Activities, Case Study of MIE PLC

Promotional Plan, Promotional Objectives, Promotional Budgeting and Promotional Mix

VDM Verlag Dr. Müller

Impressum/Imprint (nur für Deutschland/ only for Germany)

Bibliografische Information der Deutschen Nationalbibliothek: Die Deutsche Nationalbibliothek verzeichnet diese Publikation in der Deutschen Nationalbibliografie; detaillierte bibliografische Daten sind im Internet über http://dnb.d-nb.de abrufbar.

Alle in diesem Buch genannten Marken und Produktnamen unterliegen warenzeichen-, marken- oder patentrechtlichem Schutz bzw. sind Warenzeichen oder eingetragene Warenzeichen der jeweiligen Inhaber. Die Wiedergabe von Marken, Produktnamen, Gebrauchsnamen, Handelsnamen, Warenbezeichnungen u.s.w. in diesem Werk berechtigt auch ohne besondere Kennzeichnung nicht zu der Annahme, dass solche Namen im Sinne der Warenzeichen- und Markenschutzgesetzgebung als frei zu betrachten wären und daher von jedermann benutzt werden dürften.

Coverbild: www.ingimage.com

Verlag: VDM Verlag Dr. Müller Aktiengesellschaft & Co. KG
Dudweiler Landstr. 99, 66123 Saarbrücken, Deutschland
Telefon +49 681 9100-698, Telefax +49 681 9100-988
Email: info@vdm-verlag.de

Herstellung in Deutschland:
Schaltungsdienst Lange o.H.G., Berlin
Books on Demand GmbH, Norderstedt
Reha GmbH, Saarbrücken
Amazon Distribution GmbH, Leipzig
ISBN: 978-3-639-27099-0

Imprint (only for USA, GB)

Bibliographic information published by the Deutsche Nationalbibliothek: The Deutsche Nationalbibliothek lists this publication in the Deutsche Nationalbibliografie; detailed bibliographic data are available in the Internet at http://dnb.d-nb.de.

Any brand names and product names mentioned in this book are subject to trademark, brand or patent protection and are trademarks or registered trademarks of their respective holders. The use of brand names, product names, common names, trade names, product descriptions etc. even without a particular marking in this works is in no way to be construed to mean that such names may be regarded as unrestricted in respect of trademark and brand protection legislation and could thus be used by anyone.

Cover image: www.ingimage.com

Publisher: VDM Verlag Dr. Müller Aktiengesellschaft & Co. KG
Dudweiler Landstr. 99, 66123 Saarbrücken, Germany
Phone +49 681 9100-698, Fax +49 681 9100-988
Email: info@vdm-publishing.com

Printed in the U.S.A.
Printed in the U.K. by (see last page)
ISBN: 978-3-639-27099-0

Z41.00

Assessment of Promotional Activities, Case Study of MIE PLC

ACKNOWLEDGEMENTS

It is not exaggerated to state that without insisting the Almighty God, Jesus Christ, would not have been in a position to finalize this work successfully. So, primarily, I want to forward my special thanks to God.

I would like to express heartfelt appreciation and gratitude to my principal advisor, Dr. Yassin Ibrahim and co-advisor Ato Gebrehiwot Gebremariam for their valuable advice, constant support, dedication, encouragement, valuable guidance, ingenious and suggestion. In fact, this work would not have come in its present form had it not been complemented by their proper follow-up in reshaping and organizing.

I am also indebted to staff members of Mesfin Industrial Engineering PLC in Sales and Promotion, Public Relations, Finance, and Business Development Departments for their friendly cooperation, arranging for discussion and provided valuable information concerning the work.

At last but not the least, it is my pleasure to forward my special appreciation to my family and all my friends for their valuable support, nice cooperation, encouragements, and patience throughout my work.

Yemane Gidey
Mekelle University, Tigrai, Ethiopia

i

LIST OF TABLES

LIST OF FIGURES

ACRONYMS AND ABBREVIATIONS

Ads- Advertisements

B2B- Business to Business

B2C- Business to Customer

Dept- Department

DGM- Deputy General Manager

EFFORT- Endowment Fund for the Rehabilitation of Tigrai

GM- General Manager

HR- Human Resource

MIE PLC-Mesfin Industrial Engineering Private Limited Company

MR- Management Representatives

PR- Public Relation

QMS- Quality Management System

RQ- Research Question

TV- Television

USP- Unique Selling Proposition

4ps- Marketing mix elements, which is a combination of; Product, Price, Place, and Promotion.

1. INTRODUCTION

The introductory chapter begins by presenting the background to the problem area and is following by a discussion of the problem. From that, research questions and the purpose of the work *are formulating. The chapter finalizes by presenting limitation of the work.*

1.1 Background of the Work

The Ethiopian economy is an agrarian economy in which the livelihood of about 85% of the population directly or indirectly depends on the agricultural sector. The sectoral structure of the value-added to the national economy in 2004 (GDP composition of sectors) is:

- Agriculture 47%
- Service Sector 40.6%
- Industry 12.4%

Out of the total share of the industry sector, manufacturing represents 7%. Major industrial sub-sectors are food, beverage, tobacco, textiles, leather, printing, paper, and non-metallic minerals. In consumer goods manufacturing food, beverage, textile, leather and shoe dominate the large and medium scale manufacturing sub-sector in Ethiopia. These four groups, including the chemical process industries, account for 78% of the gross value of output of the large and medium scale-manufacturing sector. Obviously the metallic manufacturing industries account only less than 22% of the manufacturing sector; EEA, (2003/04)

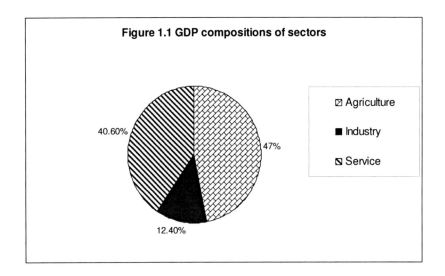

Figure 1.1 GDP compositions of sectors

40.60%

47%

12.40%

☒ Agriculture

■ Industry

☒ Service

Source: EEA, (2003/04)

Organizations exist to attain certain mission for undefined period of time. In order to exist in the business for a long period of time, organizations must look for effective and efficient ways of doing business activities to achieve organizational objectives. At present due to environmental dynamism and competitiveness, the struggle for survival and succeeding in the business has become more difficult and challenging (Rajasekhara, 2008).

Mesfin (2007) stated that, the Ethiopian manufacturing industries are operating today in a business environment characterized by dynamic environment where global competition and technological advancements are changing rapidly. In order to respond to this fast environmental change and being able to be competent in the face of stiff competition, proper implementation of marketing mix, specifically marketing promotion is important for the firms.

Promotion is one of the key aspects of the marketing mix (the other three elements are product, price, and place). Promotion keeps the product in the minds of the customer and helps stimulate demand for the product. Kotler, *et al* (2005) mentioned that, a company's total marketing communication mix– also called its promotion mix– consists of the specific blend of advertising, personal selling, sales

2

promotion, public relations and direct marketing that the company uses to pursue its promotion and marketing objectives. Thus, the company needs to effectively utilize all its promotional mix in a manner that a strength of one is use to offset the weakness of other to achieve its organizational goals and objectives, this can be done through appropriate promotional plan (Belch, *et al*, 1993).

Promotional plan provides the frame-work for developing, implementing, and controlling the organization's promotional activities and programs. Promotional planning is best viewed as a dynamic process, as it is generally evolves over a period of time and involves interactions among company personnel as well as with external parties such as advertising agencies, public relation, and marketing research firms, and consultants (Belch, *et al*, 1993).

Effective promotion bases on a sound understanding of the communication process, through reminding, informing and persuasive process. This initiates a process within a person which creates motivation, in turn leading to a particular desired course of action. After the company gains an understanding of the company communication process, and what to transmit, it is ready to develop an overall promotion plan. Such a carefully designed promotional plan consists of objectives, budgeting and promotional mix to its target segment (Belch, *et al*, 1993).

Objectives of promotion can be to introduce, inform, or remind. Company's promotional objectives can be divided in to two general categories: one is stimulating demand and the other is enhancing company image. The elements used to accomplish organization's promotional objectives are often referred to as the promotional mix (Belch, *et al*, 1993).

1.2 Statement of the Problem

Promotion keeps the product in the minds of the customer and helps stimulate demand for the product (Kotler, *et al*, 2005). Alternatively, promotion is any form of communication used to inform, boost demand, persuade or remind people about an organization or individual goods, services, image and ideas to facilitate exchange (Kotler, 1996). A carefully promotional plan consists of target audiences, objectives, budgeting and promotional mix (Belch, *et al*, 1993). Thus, a carefully planned business to business (B2B) promotion program contributes to increased efficiency and effectiveness of the overall marketing strategy of the industrial firm (Steven, 1997). However, as the information obtained from

3

the preliminary assessment, MIE PLC gives less emphasis for promotional activities and for the techniques used to devise the promotional budget.

The elements used to accomplish organization's promotional objectives are often referred to as the promotional mix and include advertising, personal selling, sales promotion, public relation and direct marketing (Kotler, *et al*, 2005). Each promotional mix has its own strengths and weaknesses, thus the company needs to effectively utilize all its promotional mix in a manner that a strength of one is use to offset the weaknesses of the other (Belch, *et al*, 1993). There are several factors that need to be considered in establishing an appropriate promotional mix include (Jennifer, 1998); the available budget, the marketing message, the complexity of the product or service, market size and location, distribution of the product, the stage in the product life-cycle, and competition.

Hence, this work was initiated to assess promotional activities of MIE PLC by raising the following leading questions;

      a. Does the company have promotional plan?

      b. What are the company's objectives for promotion?

      c. How the company establishes promotional budget?

      d. Which promotional mix and media that the company currently applies in promotion?

1.3 Objectives of the Work

The main objective of this work was to assess the promotional activities of the case company. Furthermore, the following are the specific objectives that were addressed through out of this work;

1. To analyze the promotional plan of the company
2. To assess the company's objectives of promotion
3. To identify the promotional budget method of the company
4. To describe the promotional mix and media of the company

1.4 Significance of the Work

✓ This work attempts to discover how the company increases the demand of its products and compete with others by promotion. It is of utmost importance to examine the special features of manufacturing firms' promotional activities in order to increase the demand and compete successfully. The fact that, no comprehensive study addressing promotional aspects of the MIE has been conducted yet by any one, thus, makes worth conducting the study.

✓ It is also expected that the analysis and findings of this work will help formulate appropriate promotional measures and thus the company will have broad acceptance by users and compete successfully, moreover other similar manufacturing firms will be benefited.

✓ This work will also give insights for other interested researchers about the issue and stimulate further investigations.

✓ Finally, this work will be utmost vital to fulfill my masters degree in Business Administration/ MBA/.

1.5 Scope of the Work

As it was mentioned in the introductory part of this paper, 7% of Ethiopia's industrial sector share of the economy is manufacturing. Currently there are a number of prominent existing manufacturing industries that are able to design, manufacture and assemble bodies of fuel and dry cargo truck trailers and semi trailers, and other products. MIE is one among these manufacturing industries where this study is being conducted.

This work is limited to the promotional activities of the selected case company. That was limited to its promotional budgeting, objectives, mix, and plan. It was also limited to the year of 2004-2008.

2. REVIEW OF RELATED LITERATURE

This chapter presents the theoretical part that is the foundation for the research. Theoretical frame of reference will present significant parts from chosen literature, giving understanding in the history of promotional activities: plan, budgeting, mix and measuring the result of promotional activities.

2.1 Introduction

As Secil (1999) stated, one of the challenges facing marketing managers of industrial products and services in markets are how best to carry their sales messages to the decision makers who make the purchase decisions for their companies. To deliver messages effectively, marketing managers should carefully match the media preferences of their target markets and the audience and/or readership profiles of available media types such as television, radio, direct mail, newspapers and magazines, outdoor, and others.

Because managers of marketing industrial products face a number of unique market conditions, they must specialize their approach to serve their potential industrial customers. For instance, marketing managers generally deal with fewer buyers who buy in larger quantities. These customers are usually concentrated in limited geographic areas such as industrial parks. In addition, marketers deal with professional purchasing agents who are proficient at getting the best buyer for their companies. Moreover, these agents have the benefits of receiving input from a number of specialists within and outside their companies before making final purchase decisions. In light of the few identifiable, and concentrated potential buyers, the marketing managers of industrial products and services should prepare their communication objectives to ensure that the communication media they pick will result in strong links with their targeted industrial buyers, thus resulting in sales, image building and reputation (Engel, *et al,* 1991).

6

2.2 Promotion and Promotional Activities

Promotion has had many meanings over the years. The original connotation in Latin was "to move forward" (Engel, *et al*, 1991). Promotion is one of the most important elements of modern marketing which includes the action plan that basically intend to inform and persuade the potential customers or trade intermediaries to make a specific purchase or act in a certain manner. Modern marketing calls for more than developing a good product, pricing it attractively, and making it available to target customers (Kotler, *et al*, 2006). The authors mentioned that companies must also communicate continuously with their present and potential customers that lead every company inevitably direct into the role of communicator and promoter. Promotion consists of those activities that communicate the merits of the product or service and persuade target customers to buy it (Kotler, *et al*, 2005). For a marketer it is important (i) to determine what promotion and marketing communication activities are supposed to achieve, (ii) how the promotional activities will be conducted, (iii) media vehicles be used for the purpose, (iv) how the effectiveness or success of a campaign be evaluated, and (v) how much money should be spend in each of the areas of the promotional mix in order to be successful in the competitive business environment. The process of resolving these different demands that are placed upon organizations has made the setting of promotional objectives very complex and difficult and has been termed 'a job of creating order out of chaos' (Kriegel, 1986, cited in Jakir Hossain, 2006). Marketers need to be very careful to anticipate the surrounding business environment, competitive strategies, and require creative thinking in setting promotional objectives.

Deciding on the promotion mix is an important task for the company. After setting the promotional objectives the most important is deciding how the company will achieve the promotional objectives through implementing the promotional activities. According to Paul, (1989), the promotion mix concept refers to the combination and types of promotional effort the firm puts forth during a specified time period. The author explained that, in devising its promotion mix the firm should take into account thee basic factors; the role of promotion in the overall marketing mix, the nature of the product, and the nature of the market.

2.3 Importance of Promotion

Promotion has social, business, and economic benefits. Promotion performs an informative and education task crucial to the functioning of modern society. Promotional strategy has become increasingly important both to large and small enterprises. In this competition era, most companies simply cannot survive in the long-run market environment without promotion. With the intention that, companies must communicate with their customers as well as with the public in general. Promotion has assumed a degree of economic importance, for no other reason, it provides employment for thousands of people. More importantly, however, effective promotion has allowed society to derive benefits not otherwise available, (Boone *et, al,* 1998).

2.4 Promotional Mix and Tools

Promotion as a marketing mix component stimulates demand and enhances company image (Evans and Berman 1987, cited in Michel.). Promotion keeps the product in the minds of the customer and helps stimulate demand for the product. Kotler, *et al* (2005) mentioned that, a company's total marketing communication mix– also called its promotion mix– consists of the specific blend of advertising, personal selling, sales promotion, public relations and direct marketing tools that the company uses to pursue its promotion and marketing objectives. All promotional tools (promotional mix): must blend harmoniously into an effective communication strategy, to meet the promotional objectives.

2.4.1 Advertising

Any paid presentation and promotion of ideas, goods, or services by an identified sponsor. Examples: print ads, radio, television, billboard, brochures and catalogs, signs, in-store displays, posters, motion pictures, banner ads, and emails (Kotler, *et al*, 2006). However, B2B media are selected by target audience – the particular purchase decision participants to be reached (Michael, *et al* 1995). Advertising is bringing a product (or service) to the attention of potential and current customers. Thus, an advertising plan for one product might be very different than that for another product. Advertising is becoming an increasingly important part of industrial marketing programs. With the cost of a sales call rising dramatically, industrial marketing managers are investigating the use of more economical communication vehicles to perform tasks now assigned to salespeople (Dominique, 1980). B2B advertising contributes to increased sales efficiency. Increased expenditures on advertising lead to greater brand awareness for industrial products, which translates into larger market shares and higher profits (Michael, *et al* 1995).

Before you write your ads, you should give careful thought to your unique selling position so you know what unique features and benefits to convey and to whom. Note that a common mistake among inexperienced ad writers is to write the ad to themselves, rather than to their current and potential customers. Your ads should clearly stated the benefits (of products and services) to customers, not the benefits to you -- clearly state the ads in terms that the customer will value, for example, easy access, low cost, easy to use, reliability, etc. From a management view point: advertising is a strategic device for gaining or maintaining a competitive advantage in the market place. The two basic aspects of advertising are the message (what you want your communication to say) and the medium (how you get your message across). Advertising seeks to promote the seller's product by numerous types of media; **Brochures or flyers, Magazines, Newspapers, Posters and bulletin boards, Radio announcements, and Television ads.** Brochures can contain a great deal of information if designed well, and are becoming common methods of advertising. Magazines ads can get quite expensive. Find out if there's a magazine that focuses on your particular industry. Consider placing an ad or writing a short article for the magazine. You can get your business in the newspaper by placing ads, writing a letter to the editor or working with a reporter to get a story written about your business. Newspapers are often quite useful in giving advice about what and how to advertise. Posters can be very powerful when placed where your customers will actually notice them. But think of how often you've actually noticed posters and bulletin boards yourself. A major advantage of radio ads is they are usually cheaper than television ads, and many people still listen to the radio, for example, when in their cars. A major consideration with radio ads is to get them announced at the times that your potential customers are listening to the radio. Many people don't even consider television ads because of the impression that the ads are very expensive. They are more expensive than most of major forms of advertising, (Carter, 2009).

Each of the above mentioned advertising methods or Medias have their own strengths and weaknesses. Many companies measure the effectiveness of their advertising campaign in terms of its communication effects as how does the advertising create awareness?, provide information?, stimulate demand?, enforce brand loyalty? In fact, there are companies that measure the effectiveness of their advertising in terms of its effect on company sales. However, most agree that measuring effectiveness of advertising in terms of sales effect is difficult as there are many things to affect buying decisions other than advertising, (Paul, 1999).

9

2.4.2 Personal Selling

Personal selling include, oral presentations given by a salesperson that approaches individuals or a group of potential customers. Personal selling is often used in business to business i.e. "B2B" settings, in addition to business to consumer i.e. "B2C" scenarios in which a personal and face to face medium is required for the communication of the product. In B2B situations, personal selling is preferred if the product is technical in nature. Personal selling can compose of the use of presentations, in order to convey the benefits of a firm's good/service. As a general rule, goods that are new, technically complex, and/or expensive require more personal selling effort. In the case of pure competition (a large number of small buyers with complete market knowledge of homogenous product); there is little need for personal selling. At the other extreme, when a product is highly differentiated and marketed to consumers with imperfect knowledge of product offerings, then personal selling becomes a key factor in the promotion mix. In B2C settings, personal selling is utilized if the product requires to be tailored to the unique needs of an individual. Examples of this include car (and other vehicle) sales, financial services (such as insurance or investment), etc. Personal selling involves the following points: live, interactive relationship, personal interest, attention and response, interesting presentation, clear and thorough, (Paul, 1989).

Personal selling is one of the most expensive and, for many companies, one of the most important elements for the marketing mix, (Weitz, 1981).

2.4.3 Sales Promotion

Kotler, et al (2005) defined sales promotion as, the short-term incentives to encourage the purchase or sale of a product or service. According to the authors, samples, cash refunds, price packs, premiums, advertising specialties, patronage rewards, point-of-purchase displays and demonstrations, and contests, sweepstakes and games can be used for consumer promotion tools. Many of the tools used for consumer promotions- contests, premiums, displays – can be used as trade promotions. Alternatively, the manufacturer may offer a straight discount off the list price on each case purchased during a stated period of time (also called a price-off, off-invoice or off-list. whereas in business promotion includes many of the same tools used for consumer or trade promotions but mainly conventions and trade shows and sales contests are used for business promotions. It is important to mention here that in deciding on the tools of sales promotion, marketers need to consider the competition and cost effectiveness of each tool. The purpose of sales promotion is to supplement and coordinate advertising and personal selling;

this has become increasingly important in marketing. While advertising helps build brand image and long-term value, sales promotion builds sales volume. Business-to-Business marketers spent approximately 10 percent of their promotional budgets on sales promotion (Cahner advertising research report, 1990, cited in Belch, 1993).

These promotions include video materials (other than Films), point-of-sales materials, permanent display racks, and video tapes among others. Sales promotion seems most effective when used together with advertising. In some study, a price promotion alone produces only a 15% increase in sales volume when combined with feature advertising, sales volume increased 19%; when combined with feature advertising and a point -of - purchase display, sales volume increasing 24% (Kotler, *et al* 1999).

Exhibitions and trade shows

Most industries stage business show or exhibition annually to display new advances and technological developments in the industry. Sellers present their products and services in booths visited by interested industry members. The typical exhibitor will contact four to five potential purchasers an hour on the show floor (Michael, *et al* 1995). Industry trade shows can be a cost effective way to secure customer leads, induce new products, assess preliminary customer reactions, obtain industry exposure, develop goodwill, maintaining an image, obtain favorable publicity in local media, reach otherwise hard –to-find buyers or influencers, disseminate information about the firm, obtain orders, gather intelligence on competitors, maintain and enhance corporate morale, and service current account's problems through contacts (Donald, *et al*, 1987). Trade shows are an important but under-researched component of the promotion mix for most industrial products. Like at the shopping mall most attendees either have specific plans to buy a product in the category exhibited or at least exert some degree of influence on purchase decisions in the category. Thus trade shows could be a unique and potentially attractive industrial promotion vehicle (Srinath, *et al*, 1995).

2.4.4 Direct Marketing

Direct marketing has been defined by the Institute of Direct Marketing as: the planned recording, analysis and tracking of customer behavior to develop relational marketing strategies. The use of mail, telephone or other non-personal contact tools to communicate with or solicit responses from specific customers and prospects. Mail shots and leaflets inserted in professional magazines are used to promote information products, (Carter, 2009).

11

Direct marketing is a process where a firm uses communication channels to attain and retain consumers for its product. It is a comparatively new mode of marketing communications (when compared with forms such as advertising, sales promotions, personal selling, etc.) Direct marketing involves carefully seeking out persons within a target market, and communicating to them about the nature of a product. This process is signified by brochures sent via the mail, e-mails from companies, etc. It can also constitute the use of telemarketing, and database in order to communicate with a target market, (Rupal, 2009).

Direct mail- is commonly used for corporate image promotion, product and service promotion, sales force support, distribution channel communication, and special marketing problems (Michael, *et al* 1995). A direct mail promotion typically gains the full attention of the reader and therefore provides greater impact. Industrial buyers usually will at least scan the direct mail promotions sent to them. However, reaching top executives with direct mail may be more difficult.

Web pages -- You probably would not have seen this means of advertising on a list of advertising methods if you had read a list even two years ago. Now, advertising and promotions on the World Wide Web are almost commonplace. Businesses are developing Web pages sometimes just to appear up-to-date. Using the Web for advertising requires certain equipment and expertise, including getting a computer, getting an Internet service provider, buying (usually renting) a Website name, designing and installing the Website graphics and other functions as needed (for example, an online store for e-commerce), promoting the Website (via various search engines, directories, etc.) and maintaining the Website, (Carter, 2009).

2.4.5 Public Relations and Publicity

It is building good relation with the company's various publics by obtaining favorable publicity, building up a good corporate image, and handing or heading off unfavorable rumors, stories and events. It is used to promote products, people ideas, and activities, organizations and even nations. It can have a strong impact on public awareness at a much lower cost than advertising can. The company does not pay for the space and time in the media; (Kotler, 2004). Firms had to use PR in order to determine, develop, encourage and sustain relations with key publics relative to their competitive domain. Firms are charged with the responsibility for developing and maintaining relations with publics such as financial (city and investors), government (local, national, international), communities via social responsibility, charitable endeavors (linked to strategic considerations), general publics (targeted key consumer groups), distributors, suppliers and consumers. Public relations has become the: management function that identifies, establishes, and maintains mutually beneficial relations between an organization and its publics upon whom its success or failure depends (Kitchen, 1996). The author further explained that, PR provides opportunity for firms to strengthen brand and corporate imagery by taking up opportunities for consumers to view positive messages in media likely to be read, viewed or heard by appropriate target audiences. Public relations and publicity- programmes designed to promote and/or protect a company's image, or those of its products, including product literature, exhibitions and articles about organizations' products in professional or in-house newsletters (Jennifer, 1998). Public relations include ongoing activities to ensure the overall company has a strong public image. Public relations activities include helping the public to understand the company and its products. Often, public relations are conducted through the media, which is, newspapers, television, magazines, etc.

Sponsorship- Financial or external support of an event or person by an unrelated organization or donor is common in respect of the arts, sports and charities. Large organizations, such as major publishing groups like Reed Elsevier, or software houses, such as Microsoft, may engage in sponsorship, but public sector organizations, in education and libraries, are more likely to be the recipient of sponsorship (Jennifer, 1998). For example, many businesses sponsor football teams, allowing them to put the business name or logo on the kit and giving them good publicity. The public relations media typically used include business paper articles, trade magazines, and journals. The use of articles and press releases to provide detail on new innovations and/ or developments is common in industrial markets (Belch, 1993).

A study of industrial purchasing agents indicated that the relative importance of promotional elements varied across products. Industrial marketers communicate information about their products and services through a number of different communication channels. When allocating promotional budgets among alternative promotional tools, industrial marketers need to know which are considered more useful by current and prospective customers. Logic implies that the budget allocation decision should customers' preferences for the various promotional tools (Donald, *et al*, 1987). The authors mentioned that, personal selling is the most widely used promotional tool in industrial marketing. However, industrial advertising can supplement the efforts of salespeople and, in effect, reduce the cost per sales call. Fur there more; advertising can be used to reach individuals not normally reached by sales people. Because of the effectiveness of industrial advertising and its efficiency in promoting target audiences, advertising dollars and the number of industrial advertisers have increased steadily.

The above discussion leads the researcher to a conclusion that, a company can use any of the promotional mix or a combination of more than one mix for promoting a product. And indeed, one promotional strategy may be used to support another promotional event. For example, an organization might take out a newspaper advertisement to announce their sponsorship of a sporting event. But it depends on the nature of the product, price, customers' locations, prevailing competition, cost involved, availability of the budget for promotion, company's overall objectives etc. It is worth mentioning here, that the success of the promotional activities largely depends on the realistic selection of the promotional mix(s) and the creativity in operating the promotional activities. In addition it must be recognized that company's promotion mix is likely to change over time to reflect changes in the market competition, the product's life cycle and the adoption of new strategies.

2.5 The Role of Promotion in the Marketing Mix

An appropriate promotional mix must be created in order to meet the promotional objectives of any given promotion strategy. The possible objectives for marketing promotions may include the following; new products and new companies are often unknown to a market, which means initial promotional efforts must focus on establishing an identity. In this situation the marketer must focus promotion to: effectively reach customers, and tell the market who they are and what they have to offer. The right promotion can drive customers to make a purchase. In the case of products that a customer has not previously purchased or has not purchased in a long time, the promotional efforts may be directed at getting the customer to try the product. Promotion is one of the key 4Ps in the marketing mix and as such has a key role to play in market success. Promotion is concerned with ensuring that customers are aware of the products that the organization makes available to those customers.

More specifically, the objectives of any promotional strategy will be drawn from an appropriate mixture of the following roles of promotion (Michael, 1996) to:

- Increase sales;
- Maintain or improve market share;
- Create or improve brand recognition;
- Create a favorable climate for future sales;
- Inform and educate the market;
- Create a competitive advantage, relative to competitor's products or market position;
- Improve promotional efficiency.

2.6 Promotional Planning and Stages

Promotion is an ongoing process that requires much planning. A strategy is simply a careful plan. The effectiveness of your strategy depends on more than how much money you put into it. Effectiveness results from the thoroughness of your planning and the consistency with which you carry it out (Belch, 2000). For marketer, promotional planning is important (Kotler, et al, 2005);

☞ To determine what promotion and marketing communication activities are supposed to achieve,
☞ How the promotional activities will be conducted,
☞ Media vehicles be used for the purpose,
☞ How the effectiveness or success of a campaign be evaluated, and
☞ How much money should be spending in each of the areas of the promotional mix in order to be successful in the competitive business environment.

The list below summarizes the stages in the design of promotion strategies to support the realization of promotional objectives. In the launch of a new or re-designed or re-branded product these stages would form the steps in the planning of a promotional campaign. However, many organizations are concerned not only with specific promotional campaigns, but also with maintaining a continued awareness and positive attitude to their products. In such circumstances, while each of these stages remains important, they will not necessarily always be visited in the sequence identified below (Jennifer, 1998);

- Identify target audience;
- Determine promotion objectives;
- Design the message;

- Select communication channels;
- Establish promotional budget;
- Decide on promotional mix;
- Measure results;

2.6.1 Identification of Target Audience

The first stage is to characterize the target audience. It's important in this first step to examine and understand the needs of your target market: who is your message going out to, (Laura, 2009). This target audience may include the complete market segment for the product or the organization, or a specific promotional strategy may be targeted more narrowly at a niche within the broader segment. Messages and channels may be selected accordingly, but care must be taken to ensure that other groups in the market segment are not alienated by the messages that might be associated with a niche strategy. The characteristics of the audience need to be understood. Segmentation might be applicable here, but in addition it will be important to garner an understanding of the types of marketing messages to which the audience is likely to be susceptible (for example, is quality or price a priority?) and to be aware of the audience's current image of the company and its products.

2.6.2 Determining Promotional Objectives

Promotion as a marketing mix component stimulates demand and enhances company image (Evans and Berman 1987, cited in Michel, 1995). The most obvious objective marketers have for promotional activities is to convince customers to make a decision that benefits the marketer (of course the marketer believes the decision will also benefit the customer). For most for-profit marketers this means getting customers to buy an organization's product and, in most cases, to remain a loyal long-term customer. For other marketers, such as not-for-profits, it means getting customers to increase donations, utilize more services, change attitudes, or change behaviour.

However, marketers must understand that getting customers to commit to a decision, such as a purchase decision, is only achievable when a customer is ready to make the decision. Customers often move through several stages before a purchase decision is made. Additionally before turning into a repeat customer, purchasers analyze their initial purchase to see whether they received a good value, and then often repeat the purchase process again before deciding to make the same choice.

The type of customer the marketer will attempting to attract and which stage of the purchase process a customer is in will affect the objectives of a particular marketing communication effort. And since a marketer often has multiple simultaneous promotional campaigns, the objective of each could be different.

In B2B promotion, companies have marketing objectives they wish to accomplish and they establish promotional objectives as a means for attaining these goals. The common promotional objectives will be one or more a mixture of the following (Belch, 2000, cited in Kristofer, 2007);

Creating or improved brand awareness; this objective is to improve your brand or company in the eyes of the customer, to associate good feeling with the company.

Increase sales; this objective is to get more customers to buy your product or services, or get existing customers to buy more.

Maintain or improve market share; this objective is all about holding your part of the market or increase the market share by strengthen the company on the market.

Create favorable climate for future sales; this objective is closely tied to the one above and involves persuading the market to have good impressions of your brand and company. That will make future product launches much easier.

Create competitive advantage; this objective refers to creating competitive advantage, relative to either competitor's product or market positions.

Inform and educate the market; this objective is not about increase sales or market share, but instead focusing or informing the market about changes. It can be changes in the company, legislation changes or everything else that the company wants to inform the market about.

2.6.3 Designing the Message

Each communication strategy must have a message that is consistent with its communication objectives. The message will often strongly reflect the USP of the products. The USP is the unique set of benefits which the producer believes are provided by the product, and which will be of interest to their customers. Where promotion focuses on a brand or corporate image or identity, this will form the basis of the marketing message. Another factor that needs to be taken into account is message consistency between different campaigns. An organization needs to promote a consistent, if evolving

17

image through all of its separate campaigns, otherwise the audience will become confused and no overall clear message will be communicated. The elements of the message that need to be considered are: (Jenifer, 1998).

- Content - what to say;
- Structure - how to say it logically;
- Format - how to say it symbolically;
- Source - who should say it, or act as the spokesperson.

2.6.4 Selecting Promotion Channels

In the first step of planning you should have defined the markets, products, and environments. This information will assist you in deciding which communication channels will be most beneficial (Laura, 2009). Promotional or Communication channels can be divided into personal communications and non-personal communications.

Personal communications channels are those in which two or more people communicate with one another, and word of mouth is the primary means of communication, although other media, such as e-mail are growing in significance. The most common type of personal communication channels is advocate channels, such as company sales people. Exhibitions are an important arena in which advocate channels, such as salespeople, can come into contact with customers. These are widely used in business-to-business promotion. In this context, as in many others, personal conversation will be supplemented by leaflets, posters, and possibly videos and samples (such as sample discs).

Non-personal communication channels are those in which communication is through some other medium other than person-to-person. These include:

- The press including national and regional newspapers and magazines, but most significantly for the information industry, trade, professional and technical journals.
- Television, including satellite and cable television. The expensive nature of this medium means that it is only an option for major advertisers.
- Radio offers a wide range of competitively priced promotional options. In general it is deemed to have less potential impact than television since there is no visual image.

18

- Posters can be placed in a wide variety of different environments from billboards at the roadside, to the underground and other public places, to libraries and notice boards with organizations.
- Leaflets and publicity are important "takeaways" that can act as reminders of products and contact points.

Selection criteria for promotional Media or channels

Each promotional mix has different promotional tools. It is worth mentioning here that, the success of the promotional activities largely depends on the realistic selection of the promotional tool(s) and the creativity in operating the promotional activities. Choosing between these various alternative media is difficult and center on several factors; such as media habits of the target audience, product attributes, price competition, etc.

2.6.5 Establishing the Budget

Each company brings much experience and thought to setting budgets and making plans for marketing promotions. However, to a large degree, these decisions are based on impressions rather than facts. Very little qualified intelligence exists on the relation of product and market characteristics to marketing expenditures for industrial products. One reason for this is that to conduct special studies for each individual product would be prohibitively expensive. There are at least three kinds of methods for allocating promotional expenditures (Garry, 1979);

Guideline method (rules of thumb) - Among the common techniques are "budget a constant percent of sales method," "match competition or competitive-parity method," i.e. for instance, 1% of sales or spend what competition spends.

The fundamental problem with percentage of sales method is that they implicitly make promotion a consequence rather than determinant of sales and profits and can easily give rise to dysfunctional policies (Michael, *et al* 1995).

"Objectives" (task) method- it tries to relate promotional expenditures or costs to the objectives it is accomplished. This method is applied by evaluating the tasks to be performed by promotion, analyzing the costs, associated with each task, and summing up the total costs in order to arrive at a final budget (Gary, 1979). Using the task approach, managers will allocate all the funds necessary to accomplish a specific objective, rather than allocate some arbitrary percentage of sales. The most common troubling

19

problem of this method is that management must have some instinct for the proper relationship between expenditure level and communication response.

Explicit modeling and/or experimentation- This approach attempts to relate marketing actions to profit or other objectives via theory and direct measurement. Explicit modeling and experimentation are generally expensive.

Alternatively to the above methods; the following are also potential approaches to the calculation of a promotional budget (Jennifer, 1998).

- Affordable; many companies set the promotion budget at they think the company can afford. This method completely ignores the role of promotion as an investment and the immediate impact of promotion on sales volume.
- The budget is set as a percentage of sales;
- The budget is set on the basis of seeking to achieve "share-of-voice" parity with competitors;
- The budget is set as the result of an analysis of the desired objectives, and the tasks required achieving those objectives.

2.6.6 Deciding on the Promotional Mix

This is where you will need to allocate resources among the various mixes (Laura, 2009).The promotional mix will normally include a selection of strategies from more than one of the following: advertising, direct marketing, sales promotion, public relations and publicity, personal selling and sponsorship. Each of the above components of the promotional mix has strengths and weaknesses. There are several factors that should be taken into account in deciding which, and how much of each tool to use in a promotional marketing campaign (Carter, 2009): The factors that determine the type of promotional tools are;

1. Resource availability and the cost of each promotional tool- Advertising (particularly on television and in the national newspapers can be very expensive). The overall resource budget for the promotional campaign will often determine which tools the business can afford to use.

2. Market size and concentration- If a market size is small and the number of potential buyers is small, personal selling may be the most cost-effective promotional tool. A good example of this would be businesses selling software systems designed for supermarket retailers. On the other hand, where markets are geographically disperse or, where there are substantial numbers of potential customers, advertising is usually the most effective.

3. Customer information needs- Some potential customers need to be provided with detailed, complex information to help them evaluate a purchase (e.g. buyers of equipment for nuclear power stations, or health service managers investing in the latest medical technology). In this situation, personal selling is almost always required. On the other way, Kotler *et al*, (1999) stated that customers information need depends on their readiness stage as a result promotional tools vary at different stages of buyers' readiness. Further he stated that, advertising and public relations play the most important role in the awareness building stage. Customers' conviction stage is mostly influenced by personal selling. Closing the sales is influenced by   personal selling and sales promotion and finally reordering is also influenced by personal selling and sales promotion and somewhat by reminder advertising. More specifically, the factors that need to be considered in establishing an appropriate promotional mix include (Jennifer, 1998); the available budget, the marketing message, the complexity of the product or service, market size and location, distribution of the product, the stage in the product life-cycle, and Competition.

2.6.7 Measuring Promotion Results

The evaluation of B2B promotion is demanding a complex, but absolutely essential (Michael, 1995). Budgetary constraints are generally the limiting factors. Professional research companies are often called on to develop field research studies. The author in his book also explained that, when determining the impact of advertising on moving a decision participant from an awareness of the product or company to a readiness to buy, the evaluations will usually measure knowledge, recognition, awareness, preference, and motivation.

The author further stated that, promotion involves considerable investment. It can frequently be difficult to differentiate between the effect of promotion and the other elements of the marketing mix. Nevertheless, it is important to monitor the effects of promotion, by looking at sales figures and conducting research or any measures of reputation that are available.

Measuring the promotional result can be takes place through; conducting research by measuring customers' awareness, memory, recognition, and recall power to the product/ brand or the company.

The other alternative way is sales effect by making a comparison between the pre and post promotion sales volume, (Laura, 2009).

As it is very important and decisive to evaluate the effectiveness of any business activity so does to evaluate the effectiveness of marketing communications elements. The main thing here is that how can we evaluate the effectiveness of these marketing communication tools, (Rajasekhara, 2008).

3. MATERIALS AND METHODS

This chapter presents site selection and area description of the work. i.e. case company, MIE PLC. It begins with the background history of MIE PLC. It follows description of the company's various activities, current performance. The chapter finalizes by presenting the methods and techniques of the work. i.e. nature of the study, sampling technique, data collection procedures, data analysis and organization of the work.

3.1 Profile of Mesfin Industrial Engineering PLC

3.1.1 Background of Mesfin Industrial Engineering PLC

Mesfin Industrial Engineering (MIE) PLC was established in 1993 as the engineering way of the endowment fund for the rehabilitation of Tigrai (EFFORT) companies. It is located at the northern part of Ethiopia, in the Tigrai provincial capital, Mekelle which is far around 780 km from Addis Ababa. Its manufacturing plant covers a total area of $120,000m^2$. It was initially founded with a paid capital of Br. 7 million. Starting its activity by giving maintenance services of vehicles & small-scale shop floor duties, pertaining to its long time vision & implementation strategies, it is now the leading equipment manufacturing and industrial engineering company in the East Africa. It designs and installs equipments and components for the energy, mining, manufacturing, construction, transportation, and agricultural sectors. A wide range of products is manufactured at its industrial complex, which is fully equipped with the state of the art machinery. Within its industrial complex, MIE has the full capacity to manufacture and erect hydraulic power components such as penstocks, steel liners, gate liners, gates, turbine elements & transmission. Its material testing laboratory provides radiographic, ultrasonic & other tests (Company profile 2007).

Currently MIE has 846 total number of employees. Out of this number 520 are permanent and 326 workers of different qualifications are also employed by the company as contract and sub-contract employees. It has a current capital of 228million.

3.1.2 Scope of MIE (Company brochure, 2006)

MIE in the transport industry

MIE designs and manufactures vehicle bodies, trailers, high and low-bed semi trailers as well. MIE has a capacity of manufacturing over 1500 trailers and semi trailers per annum.

MIE in the energy sector

MIE has a full capacity of manufacturing and erecting hydroelectric components. It has a unique rolling machine in East Africa that produces very large fuel storage tanks.

MIE in the industrial project

With the support of CAD and CAM software MIE designs, manufactures and erects industrial components for cement, textile, brewery, food and sugar industry. Moreover, MIE manufactures multi-purpose industrial cranes and boilers.

MIE in the construction industry

MIE manufactures a wide range of mobile and stationary crashing plants for the domestic and export market. It also manufactures concrete batching plants, trans-mixers, tippers and other similar construction equipments. Furthermore it manufactures steel bridge and constructs steel buildings.

3.1.3 Vision, Mission, Values, and Sources of Competitive Advantage for MIE

(Company profile, 2007)

Vision: To be a fully-fledged 'best in class' engineering company in the electro-mechanical and manufacturing sector.

Mission: Creating superior value to owners, customers and employees and be a pioneer in the industrialization of the nation.

Values:

1. Executing all works in a genuine, transparent and accountable manner.
2. Adding value, handle company property with maximum care and ensure efficient utilization of resources.
3. Giving full customer satisfaction and strive to exceed their expectations.
4. Working hard to be best in class and lead the way for quality.
5. Building sustainable, closer, long-lasting relationship with customers and partners.
6. Always giving maximum respect to employees, customers and partners.
7. Ensuring employment; promotion and reward are based on merit, competence and performance.
8. As the employees are the company's main sources of competitive advantage, the company therefore will create opportunities for continuous employee development and empowerment.
9. Developing brotherhood among the employees.
10. Always ensuring safe working conditions to all employees.
11. Providing necessary support to employees as much as possible.
12. Always observing the law

Sources of Competitive Advantage

- Professional, highly skilled and committed work force
- Excellent reputation
- Partner of first choice for government and reputed international companies
- Acquirement of up-to-date equipment and production machines

3.1.4 Products of MIE

Generally MIE PLC products are the following (Company profile, 2007)

I. The Product Mix of the Company is:

- o _ 3-axle draw bar dry cargo truck-trailer
- o _ 3-axle dry cargo semi-trailer
- o _ 2-axle dry cargo semi-trailer
- o _ Low bed-60 ton
- o _ 3-axle draw fuel cargo truck trailer

- o   _ 3-axle fuel cargo semi- trailer
- o   _ Dump Truck-Afro & Miller type (10m3, 14m3)
- o   _ Antenna must (up to 60 meter height)
- o   _ Underground and over ground tanker
- o   _ Crusher (25-100 t/h)
- o   _ Petroleum Reservoirs tanks (5000m3-5600m3)
- o   _ Overhead crane (10t, 5t, 2t)
- o   _ Bus body (40+1, 60+1 seat)

II. Services Rendered by MIE

i. Electromechanical erection services

- Supply and erection of pre engineering buildings & towers
- Installation of machines and equipment
- Erection of petroleum reservoir tanks capacity of 5,600m3 with electrical and instrumentation
- Erection and installation of HVAC system
- Installation of digital congress network, audiovisual system, stage lighting and machinery installation.

ii. Renting of vehicles & machinery services

_ Afro-damp truck-10m3 capacities

_ Crane 50-ton capacity

iii. Maintenance of vehicle services

- Light vehicle maintenance-Toyota, Nissan
- Heavy vehicle maintenance-Afro Truck

3.1.5 Organizational Structure

The General Manager of MIE PLC is appointed by the chairman of the board of Directors. Hierarchically, the General Manager is accountable to the Chairman of the board or corporate management. Generally, the company has sixteen (16) departments that are under the supervision of different positions (Company profile, 2007). There are eight (8) different activities that are directly reported to the general manager; namely;

- DGM Operations & Engineering
- DGM Projects
- DGM Marketing
- DGM Services
- MR for QMS and quality assurance
- Internal audit service
- Legal service
- Planning & Information Technology Department Manager

DGM represents- Deputy General Managers that mainly deal with conceptual activities to support the General Manager. Within each DGM there are various departments.

The departments under DGM Operations & Engineering are;
- Design & Technology
- Manufacturing
- Electro-Mechanical Work
- Industrial Maintenance
- Equipment Maintenance & Repair

The departments under DGM marketing are;
- Public Relations Service
- Sales & promotion
- Business development

The departments under DGM services are;
- Finance
- Supply
- Human Resource

3.1.6 Promotional Activities of MIE PLC

Three years before (in 2006/2007), the Company establishes PR department. From that onwards, this department is responsible for the promotional and communicational activities, evaluating promotional programs, and publicity programs and activities such as clarification the firm's point of view on health or environmental issues to community or interest groups.

3.2 Research Methodology and Techniques

3.2.1 Nature of the Work

There are three types of research designs for marketing studies (Churchill, *et al*, 2005): exploratory research, descriptive research and causal research. Since the purpose of the work was to assess and describe the promotional activities and practices of MIE, for this work the descriptive research design was administered and is the most relevant. Similarly, this project work was based on single company the structure of collecting the data was also based on a single case study approach. Case study is the form of descriptive research. It gathers a large amount of information about one or few participants (Thomas, *et al*, 2005).

3.2.2 Sources of Data and Methods of Data Collection

According to (Seaton, *et al*, 2000), data collected for research can be distinguished according to secondary and primary types. Secondary data are data which already exist for an established purpose. On the other hand, primary data are data not available in a secondary form and must be collected to address the specific needs of the research (Stevens, *et al*, 2008). For this study, data were collected by choosing the right respondents, professionals and it was also based on well-known literature reviews.

According to Yin, 1994 (cited in Aman Hailemariam), interviews are the most important way of collecting data when conducting case studies. An interview is an interaction between an interviewer and a respondent; the interview could be conducted through telephone or by person. When specific and in-depth data is needed then interviews are the ultimate data collection method. Due to the nature of the study, neither proven tests nor models were available. Therefore a structured interview composed of both an open-ended and closed-ended questions was administered to collect the primary data from the selected sample. The total interview questions are displayed in the appendix part.

The interview was conducted personally and questions were asked according to the interview guide which covers a total of 80 questions (attached in the Appendix part) that was prepared in advance.

These 80 questions were divided among the four respondent departments (sample of the study) as displayed in appendix part. Different individuals (including department heads and experts) were interviewed from each department. Generally, the interview was carried out in the form of discussion at department level. The researcher conducted the interview with each department on different days. This makes him to take an initiative and free of stress to collect and take notes attentively during the discussion.

The main issues that would be discussed during the interview were sent in advance before the actual interview was conducted. This was to give time to be prepared with accurately and well motivated answers. During the interview the researcher took notes. The interviewees spoke Tigrigna; as a result the researcher tried to translate some interview questions in to their mother tongue Tigrigna to get a relaxed atmosphere during the actual interview. The researcher knew that they could speak English and that the paper would also be written in English and the researcher could also have saved time if he interviewed them in English but may be would not have got the same accurate and well motivated answers. The second source of data for this project work was secondary data source. To collect secondary data, company annual reports, brochures, magazines, books and journals were consulted.

3.2.3 Population and Sample of the Work

Since the study was conducted on organizational base, particularly MIE PLC, all departments of the company were considered as total population for the study. As it was mentioned in the above sections, the company has sixteen (16) departments. From this number, four (4) departments constituting 25% of the total population of the study were purposively selected as sample size for collecting data on the promotional aspects of the company. Namely: sales and promotion department, public relations department, finance department, and business development department were the selected respondents. Out of the four respondent departments, three departments, namely; sales and promotion, public relations and business development were from deputy general manager (DGM) marketing. The only department from deputy general manager (DGM) services was finance department. It is important to note here that, three individuals from Sales and Promotion department, two individuals from Finance department, one person from Public Relations department, and one person from Business Development department have been interviewed.

29

The type of sampling design that was administered for selecting sample size was purposive (judgmental) sampling. The reason for administering this type of sampling design was the study title was directly related to these functional areas so that the researcher hopes that the individuals in these departments could provide more relevant data for the study.

3.2.4 Methods of Data Analysis

Due to the nature of the study, neither proven tests nor models were available. Therefore, a structured interview was designed to answer the research questions. Data were collected by choosing the right respondents and professionals. Responses of the respondents interviewed were analyzed to gain insights in to qualitative aspects. To analyze the quantitative data, simple statistics applying Microsoft excel application were consulted.

3.2.5 Organization of the Work

The whole discussion of the study is outlined in a systematic way and will be presented in six different chapters. It introduces by the first chapter, which covers justification of the study, objectives, significance of the study and methodology. The second chapter presents review of the theoretical and related literatures. Company background and profile will be presented in the third chapter. Data are going to be presented in the fourth chapter. The fifth chapter presents the analysis and discussion part of the study. Finally, the last chapter will cover conclusions and recommendations of the whole discussion of the study.

Figure 3.1 outline of the project Work

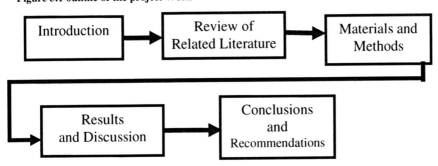

4. RESULTS AND DISCUSSION

This chapter presents the empirical data of both primary and secondary data. The data obtained from the various sources are presented in a systematic way by grouping similar interview questions under the same section in accordance with the research questions. The analysis and discussion part in comparison with the existing theories are also presented in this chapter. Since this chapter is a base to reach at certain conclusions, the analysis will be made in accordance to the research questions.

4.1 RQ-1: Does the Company have Promotional Plan?

Promotional Plan

In this section analysis concerning the first research question will be discussed and presented. As of the response of most interviewees, the company has a promotional plan which was prepared by PR department. The PR department prepared annual promotional plan and an action plan for its implementation. In addition, the annual plan for the implementation of PR and promotional tasks (attached in the appendix) shows, the company's promotional plan incorporates the promotional mix and media; TV advertisement, news paper advertisement, quarterly news letter, gift materials, exhibition and trade fairs, stickers, promotional film and photos, bill board, and website advertisement in the year 2008 (annual company promotional plan of 2008). This document further stated, TV advertisement was planned to be conducted in selected holidays; Id Al Adha, Ethiopian Christmas, Adwa's victory, Meulid, and Ginbot 20. Further the company also planned to participate in trade exhibitions of the 12th Addis Chamber International Trade Fair, Energy Expo (ENEXPO), AGRIHORTEC, 5th International Automotives Fair (IAF), which were prepared in advance.

According to Kotler, *et al,* 2005, promotion is one of the most important element of modern marketing which includes the action plan. In addition, according to Belch (1993), promotion is an ongoing process that requires much planning. A carefully promotional plan consists of target audiences, objectives, budgets, and promotional mix. However, the company's promotional plan incorporates objectives, promotional mix and tools that match the Jennifer, (1998) theory. But it shows nothing about target audiences and measuring and evaluation of the results of promotion, which are the first and the last steps respectively in preparing promotional plan, in which the company deviates from the theory. In preparing the promotional plan Jennifer, (1998) stated, the characteristics of the audience need to be understood, so that messages and channels can be selected accordingly.

As of the responses of most interviewees, the company lacks effective target audience identification while preparing the promotional plan. Or to whom the promotion is made was not clearly stated in the company's promotional plan. This indicates that, the company did not understood and considered the types of marketing messages to which the audience was likely to be susceptible (for example, is quality or price a priority?) and to be aware of the audience's current image of the company and its products. As a result, all the target audiences were expected to obtain similar promotional messages. Generally, the company's promotional strategy lacks target audiences identification.

It is important to monitor the effects of promotion, by looking at sales figures and any measures of reputation that are available. Laura, (2009) stated, after marketing communications are assigned; the promotional plan must be formally defined in a written document. In this document, determine how you will measure the effectiveness once it is implementing should be included. However, as all the interviewees agreed that, the company's promotional plan didn't incorporate ways of measuring the result of promotion. From this the researcher can interpret, it was not formally known by the company whether the promotional messages reached to target audiences and met the expected result. In other words, once the company develops and sends its promotional message to target audiences: whether the target audiences recognized or recall the promotional messages, what they remember about the message, how they felt about the message, and whether their attitudes towards the company were affected by the message were not assessed.

In forwarding opinions regarding the effectiveness of the promotional activities that the company undertakes: interviewees from Finance Department strongly argued that the company's promotional activity as effective. On the other hand, interviewees from Sales and Promotion Department and PR Department strongly argued the promotional activity of the company as difficult to state as effective or ineffective. This is because; the company has no formal promotional measurement which was incorporated in its promotional plan. Finally, interviewee from Business Development Department said that, the company's promotional activity was ineffective because the company's promotional plan by it self lacks effective marketing research conduct while it was prepared. But, all interviewees strongly underline for the importance and need of promotional impact assessment in the company. They agreed promotional impact assessment as essential for the company. Therefore, as response of most interviewees indicates, the result of the company's promotional activities will be easily identifiable and measurable if it develops or designs various promotional impact assessment mechanisms.

The over all analysis regarding the promotional plan of the company leads the researcher to conclude that: the company has a promotional plan, but target audiences identification and measuring the result of promotional activity were not effectively recognized and considered while preparing the plan. In addition, as majority of the interviewees replied, the company's promotional activity was an effective as a result it needs effective ways of measurement.

4.2 RQ-2: What are the Company's Objectives for Promotion?

In this section analysis concerning the second research question will be discussed and analyzed. There are different theories about promotional objectives. But, in this paper the Belch, (1993) theories will be used for analysis and discussion purpose.

Promotional Objectives

Belch, (1993) stated, setting promotional objectives is important for three main reasons; objectives provide a means of communication or promotion and coordination, act as a guide for decision making, provide a benchmark so that relative success or failure of a program can be determined. According to Belch, 2001(cited in Kristofer Ejebro, 2007), the common promotional objectives will be one or more a mixture of the following different objectives; increase sales, creating or improved brand awareness, maintain or improve market share, create favorable climate for future sales, inform and educate the market, and create competitive advantage; the following table (Table 4.1) represents the responses of the interviewees regarding promotional objectives of the company.

33

Table 4.1 Promotional Objectives

Common Promotional Objectives	Company's Objective
Increase Sales	✓
Creating or Improved Company Image	✓
Maintain or Improve Market Share	✓
Create Favorable Climate for Future Sales	✓
Create Competitive Advantage	✓
Inform and Educate The Market	✓

✓ = Stated as Objective

As Table 4.1 shows, the company stated increase sales, creating or improved company image, maintain or improve market share, create favorable climate for future sales, create competitive advantage, and inform and educate the market as its objectives; that is, the company used marketing promotion to demonstrate its products to existing and new customers. This is to mean that, without promotion the company could not attract new customers and even keep its existing ones. The company promotes its products to keep existing customers as well as to attract new ones, which results increase in sales.

MIE has a promotional objective of creating or improved company image as replied by the interviewees. The company conducted marketing promotion to improve and build image in the eyes of the customer, to associate good feeling with the company. The company has been participating in various exhibitions and social events such as sponsoring that helped the company to build its image. In addition, interviewees from Sales and Promotion and Finance Departments said that, to mention as an experience, "There was a film program called 'Gilt' in ETV sponsored by MIE. At that time there was a miss conception regarding MIE's product particularly towards Afro car from customers in particular and the society in general. When MIE started to sponsor that film customers in particular and society in general started to change their misconception and talk favorably about MIE. From that onwards MIE has gained good image in the society."

With regard to maintain or improve market share promotional objective: the company tried to increase and maintain its market position. The company promoted its major product: trailers in their durability as a result it had obtained 80% of local market share in trailers in local market as replied by interviewees. With hope of maintaining this market share the company promoted its products to keep its existing customers and to attract new ones. As Table 4.1 shows, creating favorable climate for future sales was also another promotional objective of the company as respondents' response. The company hoped that the promotional activity creates favorable climate for future sales if it used effectively. Currently the company is on process to introduce new cars (GEELY) and it expects to advertise intensively and effectively these cars with hope of creating favorable condition for sales. From Table 4.1 the other promotional objective of the company was creating competitive advantage; this objective refers to creating competitive advantage, relative to either competitor's product or market positions. Thus, competition was also the company's promotional objective. Marketing promotional activity helped the company to compete successfully, to inform and convince customers to purchase, because promotion is the channel of information to inform customers to purchase its products more than competitors. Finally, Table 4.1 shows, the company stated inform and educate the market as its promotional objective. This objective was not about increase sales or market share, but instead focusing on informing the market about changes. It can be legislation changes or everything else that the company wants to inform the market about. Through its promotional activities people in general and customers in particular obtained information regarding what the company produces and its overall performances.

With regard to the promotional objectives of the company: the researcher can interpret that, as response of most interviewees (indicated in Table 4.1), the company needs to achieve different objectives with the help of its promotional activities that are broadly related with sales objectives and communication or building and enhancing company image. All the above mentioned company's promotional objectives are long-term so that the company could not obtain immediate effect or impact. More specifically, since the company products are technical and more expensive customers take long time purchase decision to make an actual purchase after they receive promotional messages, as a result the company could not get immediate effect or impact on its sale through its promotional activities. Generally, the company's promotional objectives are long-term, and were stated in general terms. Therefore it became extremely difficult for the company to determine what was accomplished by its promotional activities as well as to devise appropriate budget and promotional mix.

RQ-3: How the Company Establishes Promotional Budget?

In this section analysis concerning the third research question will be discussed and presented. There are different theories about methods of determining promotional budgets. The researcher used different theories to support and clarify the concept. But, for analysis purpose of this research question the

Jennifer, (1998) theories would be used. First theoretical concepts about promotional budgets and expenditure would be presented, and then company's methods of budget allocation and expenditure on promotional activities would be compared against the theory.

Promotional Budgeting

Garry, (1979) stated, each company brings much experience and thought to setting budgets and making plans for marketing promotions. However, to a large degree, these decisions are based on impressions rather than facts. Very little qualified intelligence exists on the relation of product and market characteristics to marketing expenditures for industrial products. According to him, one reason for this is that to conduct special studies for each individual product would be prohibitively expensive.

According to Jennifer (1998), the potential approaches to the calculation or determination of a promotional budget are: affordable method, the percentage of sales method, comparative parity method, and the objective task method. Table 4.2 represents respondents' response with regard to the company's method of promotional budget determination.

Table 4.2 Methods for Establishing Promotional Budget

Common Methods	Company's Method
Affordable Method	✓
Percentage of Sales	
Comparative-Parity	
Objectives and Task Method	
Others	

✓ = Stated as Method

As the above Table 4.2 shows, the company followed a method for allocating promotional budgets. In responding to a question on the method(s) of determining promotional budget, all interview respondents express that the company used only one method in doing so. Accordingly they replied that, first budget requisite was prepared by PR Department then team will discuss and finally gets approval by management. The team was a combination of different individuals with different

36

qualifications. But, about 80-90% of the team members were from Industrial, Mechanical, Electrical and other Engineering fields of study as the response of an interviewee from PR Department. This team decided the budget based on whether the amount was enough for promotion in relation to other activities. i.e. by saying this amount of birr is enough for promotion in a given year. Interviewees from PR, Sales and Promotion and Business Development Departments stated that, budgeting as the major problem associated with promotional activities of the company.

From this the researcher can interpret, it was found that the company uses the affordable method rather than the existing market demands in determining the promotion budget. The company's budgeting process did not try to relate promotional expenditures or costs to the objectives it was accomplished. In other words, the tasks to be performed by promotion were not considered in determining budget for it. This indicates the company did not consider marketing promotional activity as investment in which that requires careful analysis and appropriate fund and its immediate impact on sales volume. Whatever competitors allocate and spend on promotional activities, and the company's sales increases or decreases were not considered by the company in establishing budget for its promotional activities.

The following graph (Fig 4.1) represents the company's total actual and budgeted promotional expenditure for selected five years.

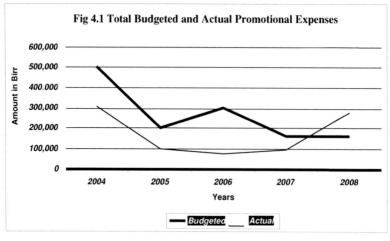

Source: *Unpublished Company's Report*

As Fig 4.1 shows, from year 2004-2005 both the budgeted and the actual amount of expenditures was declined but at different rates. From 2005 to 2006 the budgeted amount for promotion was increased but sharply declined in the year 2006. In the year 2007 and 2008 the same amount was budgeted for promotional activities. In the year 2006 very small amount was actually spent on promotion. From 2007 onwards the actual amount spend on promotion was significantly increased, even it goes above the budgeted amount in the year 2008.

Generally, from the above (Fig 4.1) the researcher can simply interpret, the budgeted amount for promotional activities was almost more than double of the actual expenses. That is, actual promotional expenses were insignificant in comparison with budgeted amount for it. As a result there was inappropriate budget utilization. But as it was mentioned in the above discussion, in the company there was a budgeting problem, which means way of determining budget for promotion. Thus, the inappropriate budget utilization could result from the inappropriate company's method of budgeting as mentioned by the interviewees. This is because, the budget for promotion was allocated and approved below the request by the team, and as a result they would be forced to compress the various tasks during implementation in line with the approved budget which leads to inappropriate performance. Therefore, the researcher insights to generalize, the company's promotional budgeting exert an influence on the performance of its promotional activities.

When interviewees were asked to express their opinion whether the current amount spent on promotion was enough or not: most interviewees realized that the current method of budgeting was not important because it approves the budget below the request with out looking and minimizing the tasks. More specifically, some interviewees were strongly agreed that, the company's current expenditure on promotional activity as enough. In contrast, the company's current expenditure on promotion is not enough to undertake effective promotional activities was forwarded by majority of the interviewees.

Therefore, as most of the respondents realized that, promotional activities need to increase, but failed to do due to the budgeting problems. But, if the company's products (existing and new) are not properly communicated to potential and current customers, no product can expect more customers to purchase. Because the nature or quality of the product not only depends on its features but also how effectively the company communicates and presents to its potential and existing customers which needs appropriate fund.

Table 4.3 Actual Promotional Expenditure Ratio to Various Items

Items	Years				
	2004	2005	2006	2007	2008
Sales	0.42	0.20	0.05	0.004	0.16
Cost of goods sold	0.48	0.22	0.07	0.06	0.20
Operating expense	4.10	0.33	0.78	0.80	1.99
Selling and distribution expenses	11.80	15.23	12.24	6.90	21.60

Source: Unpublished Company's Income Statement and Own Calculations

Table 4.3 in the above shows the actual promotional expenditure of the company in relation to other activities of the company (see Appendix-3).

As Table 4.3 shows, in the first two years 2004 and 2005, sales and promotional expenses were declining but in different rates. In general, the promotional expense of the company in the selected five years was below 1% of its sales. More specifically, the company's promotional expense to sales ratio was 0.42% in the year of 2004 and dropped to 0.20% in 2005 as its sales declined. Then in the year 2007 promotional expense was dropped down to 0.05% as sales increases significantly. As sales started to decline in 2008, the company started to gave attention for its promotional activities.

The promotional expense as measured to cost of goods sold ratio presents in Table 4.3. Cost of goods sold covers all the costs directly incurred in production. The promotional expense of the company's in the selected five years was averagely below 1% of its total cost of goods sold. Table 4.3 also shows, the promotional expenses as measured to operating expense ratio: with the exception of 2004 and 2008, it was below 1%. The total operating expenditure of the company increased from 7,501,301 to 29,802,468 in year 2004 to 2005, but the expenditure on promotion dropped down from 306,993 to 97,379 in the same year. This indicates that the company spends more amount on other than promotional activities and little amount on promotional activities. In general, the company's promotional expense covered insignificant portion from the total operating expenditures that was averagely below 1.6%.

39

Finally, Table 4.3 shows, the promotional expenses as measured to selling and distribution expenses ratio. As noted previously, the promotional expense is one among the items incorporated in selling and distribution item in the company's income statement. As a result with the exception of in the year 2008, these two items have direct relationship. This is to mean that, they increase and decrease in the same way but at different rates. But in the year 2008 the company's expenditure on promotional activities increased significantly. As of table 5.3, in the year 2004 the promotional expenditure covered only about 11% from the total selling and distribution expenditures. This indicates that the rest 89% was spend on distribution activity. In the year 2005 it was increased into 15% but dropped down into 12% and 7% in the year 2006 and 2007 respectively. Together this indicates that the company was giving more attention to its distribution activity. On the other hand, in the year 2008 the expenditure on promotion was significantly increased, which indicates that the company somewhat tried to gave attention to its promotional activities as it is shown in the following Fig 4.2.

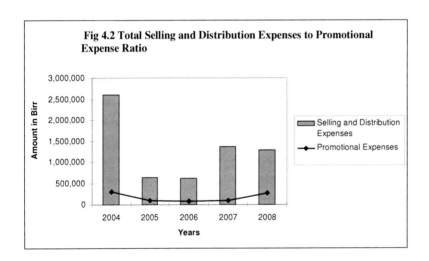

Fig 4.2 Total Selling and Distribution Expenses to Promotional Expense Ratio

Source: Unpublished Company's Income Statement and Own Calculations

Generally as it is indicated in the above Fig 4.2, the company's promotional expenses covered little portion of amount from the total selling and distribution expenses, which was averagely below 13% and the remaining 87% was spend on distribution activities.

40

The over all analysis with regard to promotional budget determination and expenditure is: the company was allocated budget for promotion using affordable method that ignores the tasks to be implemented by promotion. As a result, the company's promotional expenditure compare to other activities of the company was insignificant. Further, company's current expenditure on promotion was not enough in comparison to the tasks or objectives that are designed to achieve. Consequently, the company does not consider promotional activity as investment that requires careful analysis in determining fund for it. In addition, in comparison to other activities of the company gives less attention for promotional activity.

4.4 RQ-4: Which Promotional Mix and Media that the Company Currently Applies in Promotion?

In this section, analysis concerning the fourth research question would be discussed and presented. According to Kotler, *et al,* (2005), promotion consists of those activities that communicate the merits of the product or service and persuade target customers to buy it. Kotler, *et al* (2005) mentioned, a company's total marketing communication mix– also called its promotion mix– consists of the specific blend of advertising, personal selling, sales promotion, public relations and direct marketing tools that the company uses to pursue its promotion and marketing objectives. According to him, the industrial markets spend on personal selling, sales promotion, advertising, public relations, and direct marketing in that order. Thus, these are the common and suitable promotional mix for industrial products.

Advertising- all interview respondents have stated advertising as the current promotional mix that the company used to undertake promotional activities. Michael, *et al* (1995) stated, increased expenditures on advertising lead to greater brand awareness for industrial products, which translates into larger market shares and higher profits. The company heavily advertises for the new introduced products through TV to create awareness on target audiences. The following Table 4.4 shows the company's current advertising tools.

Table 4.4 Advertising Tools

Advertising Tools	Respondent's Response
TV	✓
Radio	✓
Printed Materials	✓
Internet	*
Others	

✓ = Stated as Current Advertising Tool

* = Stated as Potential Advertising Tool

As Table 4.4 shows, interviewees have stated TV, radio, and printed materials as the current advertising tools of the company. Internet was also important advertising tool that the company tried to practice through, but currently it was not being appropriately practiced by the company as the interviewees' response. Thus, this tool needs attention to effectively utilize in disseminating information. The company made advertisements through radio, televisions, local newspapers, selamta magazines, and other printed materials like brochures in disseminating information among the potential and existing customers in order to draw and keep customers' attention. This shows the company finds advertising as one of the most important and used promotional mix that dominated its promotional activities.

Personal Selling- majority of the interviewees selected personal selling as the current promotional mix of the company. But, some interviewees did not select personal selling and have agreed that personal selling is not being currently practiced as promotional mix by the company. Personal selling composes the use of presentations, in order to convey the benefits of the company's products and services. As a general rule, goods that are new, technically complex, and/or expensive require more personal selling effort. It is obvious that the company's products are more technically complex and expensive, as a result using personal selling as promotional mix will have unreserved benefits for the company. The company's sales officers are technically qualified and were placed as sales officers, but in addition to their normal work, they also acted as salesperson. So, this inappropriate placement affects personal selling effectiveness. According to Michael, (1995) personal selling is the most demand-stimulating force in the business marketer's promotional mix. But, the sales officers of the company simply explained and answered customers' inquiry when customers were coming to their site rather than acting as demand stimulator by articulating customers' need. Michael, (1995) also stated, the use of personal selling as promotional mix needs recruiting, selecting, training, developing, supervising, and motivating sales personnel to achieve promotional objectives of the company. But, since personal selling was expensive for the company it did not use on its proper way as forwarded by respondents. Specifically, instead of recruiting, selecting, and training individuals those are best suited to salesperson; the company used its sales officers to perform salesperson's activity in addition to their normal activities. With regard to personal selling, as the response of most interviewees indicated, the researcher can interpret that the company saw and used personal selling to enhance relationship with its customers

Sales Promotion- majority of the interviewees believed that the company currently uses sales promotion to undertake its promotional activities. But some of the interviewees did not believe sales promotion as the current promotional mix of the company. The company used the techniques of sales promotion which include gift materials, exhibition and trade fairs from the various alternatives of sales promotion techniques. Kotler, *et al* (2005) state, whereas in business promotion includes many of the same tools used for consumer or trade promotions but mainly conventions and trade shows and sales contests are used for business promotions. As the company's news letter entitled 'MESFIN NEWS LETTER' (published every three months) states: brochures, company profile which were also among promotional media of the company. In addition, the company also participated in exhibition which was conducted in Sudan in 2008 entitled 'Ethio-Sudan Trade and Cultural Fair'. The main objective of the company in that exhibition was market assessment (Company News Letter). In 2009 there was AGRI HORTEC exhibition that was conducted at Addis Ababa exhibition center. MIE was participated in that exhibition by preparing different gifts such as T-shirt, pens, and one Sonalika tractor. At that time the company used TV ads along with the (Company news letter Vol.7 No. 7 August 2009).

Generally, the company participated in exhibitions/fairs arranged internationally and locally. The company used exhibition as promotional mix to obtain potential market and promises from target audiences. With regard to sales promotion, the company's promotional activity was dominated by exhibition and trade fairs.

Public Relations- According to Kotler (2004), public relation is building good relation with the company's various publics by obtaining favorable publicity, building up a good corporate image, and handing or heading off unfavorable rumors, stories and events. Alternatively, Jennifer (1998) stated, public relations and publicity- programmes designed to promote and/or protect a company's image, or those of its products, including product literature, exhibitions and articles about organizations' products in professional or in-house newsletters. The public relations media typically used include business paper articles, trade magazines, and journals. According to Belch (1993), the use of articles and press releases to provide detail on new innovations and/ or developments is common in industrial markets.

With regard to public relations, majority of the respondents selected, public relation as current promotional mix of the company. But some respondents did not view public relations as current promotional mix of the company. As the various documents of the company indicates that, the public relations department of the company was responsible for the promotional and communicational activities and publicity programs and activities such as clarification the company's point of view on health or environmental issues to community or interest groups. In addition, the company promoted its image by sponsoring different events, making audio-visual presentations, seminars, magazines, newsletters that help to improve its image and reputation. But, the company could not effectively utilize this promotional mix because of lack of personnel as of the respondents' response.

Direct Marketing- Rupal, (2009) explained, direct marketing as a process where a firm uses communication channels to attain and retain consumers for its product. The company has developed a website and an email address to provide the information regarding the company in general and the product in particular though the web was not updated. None of the interviewees were selected direct marketing promotional mix as company's current promotional mix. According to the response of respondents, the company has still an opportunity to undertake promotional activities via its website and an email address and are essential.

The researcher's overall analysis with respect to the company's promotional mix and tools is: the company believed that almost all promotional mix important but its promotional activity was dominated by advertising as all interviewees have agreed. As the responses of the interviewees and various documents indicated, the other more practiced promotional mix of the company was sales promotion particularly exhibition and trade fairs. Kotler, (2005) recommends that, personal selling is an effective promotional mix for products that are technical, expensive and risky. But, the promotional activities undertaken by the company was dominated by advertisement that was mainly limited to

44

traditional activities like TV, radio and printed materials. Thus, the company deviates from the theoretical concepts of Kotler in utilizing appropriate promotional mix for its products.

4.5 Factors Influencing the Company's Choice of Promotional Mix

Factors that influence choice of promotional mix are going to be presented in this section. According to Carter, (2009) the promotional mix will normally include a selection of strategies from more than one of the following: advertising, direct marketing, sales promotion, public relations and publicity, personal selling. There are several factors that should be taken into account in deciding which, and how much of each mix to use in a promotional marketing campaign.

The following Table 4.5 shows the factors that influence the choice of promotional mix of the company according to the response of the interviewees;

Table 4.5 Promotional Factors

Common Promotional Factors	Company's Rate on Factors
Resource Availability and The Cost	✓
Market Size and Concentration	✓
Customer Information Needs	*
Others	✓

  ✓   = Rated as Promotional Factor

  *   = Least but Important Factor

Resource Availability and the Cost of Each Promotional Tool

According to Carter, (2009) the overall resources and budget for the promotional campaign will often determine which tools the business can afford to use. As Table 4.5 shows, respondents rated resource availability and cost of the promotional mix, i.e. budget as influential factor that the company gives emphasis in making choice among the various promotional mixes. As responses of most interviewees indicated, budgeting was the most influential factor for the company while selecting promotional mix.

45

Market size and concentration

Carter, (2009) argued that, if a market size is small and the number of potential buyers is small, then personal selling may be the most cost-effective promotional tool. On the other hand, where markets are geographically disperse or, where there are substantial numbers of potential customers, advertising is usually the most effective. As the above Table 4.5 shows, respondents rated budgeting as the company's influential factor in selecting promotional mix. In addition the company also considered market size and concentration as an influential factor. Thus, from the above mentioned factors, market size and concentration was also the other influential factor that the company took into account while selecting promotional mix.

Customer information needs

According to Carter, (2009) some potential customers need to be provided with detailed, complex information to help them evaluate a purchase. In such situations, personal selling is almost always required. Kotler *et al*, (1999) also stated, customers information need depends on their readiness stage as a result promotional tools vary at different stages of buyers' readiness. As the above Table 4.5 shows, interviewees believed customers' information need is an important factor that needs to be emphasized but currently this factor was considered as a least influential factor by the company as the interviewees forwarded. This shows, the company currently selects a given promotional mix and conducts its promotional activities with less emphasis regarding whether customers need that information or not. In other words, the right promotional message is delivered via the right promotional mix to the right customer at the right time were less considerable things by the company. Further, the company also gave less attention to customers' readiness stage while selecting a promotional mix. In addition to the above formally mentioned factors the company also gave emphasis to other essential factors such as number of people exposed to the mix, its relevance to engineering issues or company's product.

The over all responses of the interviewees with regard to promotional factors leads the researcher to conclude that: the company promotes its products and name through a given promotional mix that was selected based on several factors. Like budget, market size and concentration, number of people exposed to the mix, its relevance to engineering issues or its products, which were the most influential factors and customers' information need which was the least influential factor. The company selected a promotional mix that was more relevant to its product with little emphasis regarding whether customers were liking and aware that promotional mix. More specifically, with little consideration or with less emphasis about what information does the customer really need, when the customer needs that information and how much information that the customer needs. In other words, a promotional mix relevant to the company's product, with greater contribution and followed by large number of people or suitable to mass market as well as relatively low cost was selected by the company.

4.6 Major Problems Associated with Promotion

The promotional efforts of any product or service by any organization are intended to achieve the better performance in achieving the goal of the organization. Considering the same, it was attempted to evaluate the overall promotional activities undertaken and launched by MIE to have a clear understanding whether the company is performing in an expected way or not. Here under this section the researcher tried to mention the common promotional problems of the company and discuss what implications they would have. The common problems of the company with regard to promotional activity include the following;

Budgeting and awareness- According to Laura, (2009) budgeting is the exciting part. Company must determine the total promotion budget. This involves determining cost breakdowns per territory and promotional mix elements. Alternatively, Jennifer, (1998) stated the available budget among the several factors that need to be considered in establishing an appropriate promotional mix.

The major problems that the company faced in promotion was: budgeting; budget for promotion was approved by the team. Since the team is a combination of more technical individuals, the team members overlook promotion or lack awareness of promotion as a result they ignore the role of promotion when deciding budget for it. When the researcher was asked the team members to mention the current promotional mix of the company: they were replied differently as it was presented in promotional mix section in this paper. This indicates, the team members have not recognized and aware of the promotional activities of the company. Therefore, this awareness problem on promotion influences budget determination for it. According to Jennifer, (1998) affordable method of budgeting completely ignores the role of promotion as an investment and the immediate impact of promotion on sales volume.

As majority of the interviewees stated, there was a serious problem when deciding budget for promotion in the company. The company gave less attention for promotional activities and did not consider marketing promotion as investment that required huge capital which generates a return. In addition in the company there was a misconception regarding promotional activities that were perceived as an organization needs much promotional activities when its products are consumer products and where there are a lot of competitors. Further the company (management bodies) assumed that, promotional activities do not stimulate demand for expensive products like MIE, because the products are capital products and are produced on order-base. So that customers need more quality, timely delivered, and fair price for the products that they order in advance rather than information. Besides this, the company gave more attention and allocated enough budgets accordingly for the care of product quality, pricing activity and delivery time among the four marketing mix. While less attention and inappropriately allocated budget was given for promotional activities in comparison with the other three Ps. i.e. the company allocated budget in a way that ignores the role of promotional activities. Thus, the budgeting and awareness problem of the company on promotion influences the effectiveness of the company's promotional activities.

Personnel- it is known that achieving organizational goals are possible through enough number of enthusiastic and motivated employees. With out having enough number of employees it will be difficult for realizing organizational goals as they were expected or planned. The PR department of the company has responsibilities for the promotional and communicational activities. But, as it was raised during the discussion, this department is understaffed and is seriously influenced by this. Thus, under staffing makes the department to be incompetent in performance that exerts a negative influence on the effectiveness of company's promotional activities.

Kotler, (2005) stated, industrial markets should spend on personal selling primarily. However, the company inappropriately utilized personal selling as promotional mix that remains a lot. The company's sales managers were acting as sales people. Thus, the company's activity on using personal selling as promotional mix was not effective due to lack of enough qualified salespeople. Although these individuals were technically well equipped, they lack sales person quality and did not play sales person's role on its right way. Together the above mentioned personnel problems negatively influenced the effectiveness of promotional activities of the company.

48

Promotional impact assessment- Laura, (2009) stated, after marketing promotions are assigned, determine how company will measure the effectiveness once it is implementing. According to him, measuring the promotional result can takes place through: conducting research by measuring customers' awareness, memory, recognition, and recall power to the product/ brand or the company. The other alternative way is sales effect, by making a comparison between the pre and post promotion sales volume. As the responses of all interviewees show, the company needs to have promotional impact assessment. Even if, the company obtained responses from customers informally, the company faced difficulty to determine whether the promotional activity has a return to the company that was mainly due to absence of promotional impact assessment to measure the result of each promotional activity.

In general, the over all responses regarding the promotional problems of the company leads the researcher to conclude as: there were different problems that negatively influenced the company's promotional activities, among these the most prominent were budgeting and awareness, lack of enough qualified personnel, and inability to measure the result of the company's promotional activities.

5. CONCLUSION AND RECOMMENDATION

This final chapter presents the findings and conclusions of the work based on the analysis made on the previous chapter. Then, based on the findings forwarded possible recommendations for managerial implications and directions for further work are presented.

5.1 Introduction

Manufacturing industry is now a fastest growing industry in Ethiopia. The ever increasing growth of this industry and its market has increased the competition among the manufacturing firms. As a result, the success of any manufacturing firm depends on how well it can initiate and adopt the competitive marketing strategy over its competitors. Promotion is one of the most important element of the marketing mix through which the information regarding the over all activities of the manufacturer passes to potential and existing customers in particular and the society in general. Besides, the manufacturing firm needs to undertake effective promotional activities so as to keep and attract customers. The project work tried to assess the promotional activities of Mesfin industrial engineering/ MIE PLC. This work shows as the company give less attention for promotional activities. The major reasons for concluding in such a way are insufficient promotional measures undertaken by the company, inappropriate budgeting, lack of professionals, and inefficient use of promotional mix. So, it is essential for the concerned bodies of the company to consider these issues or limitations very carefully and on the priority basis for successful implementation of promotional activities.

5.2 Conclusions

The data collected from interviewees of four different departments administering through structured interview, the researcher's observation and various literatures have provided the means to answer the leading research questions. Based on the analysis and discussion presented in chapter four, the findings or answers for each research question are presented in the following paragraphs.

The findings of this project work suggest that the company has a promotional plan that was developed by the PR department. The company conducted promotional activities according its plan, but in some situations it undertakes promotional activities even out of its promotional plan. But, as the response of the interview respondents revealed that, target audiences identification and measuring the result of promotional activity were not effectively recognized and considered by the company while preparing the promotional plan. Thus, the company believed that measuring and controlling promotional plan is important in promotion. But due to budget problem and lack of enough number of professionals the company did not follow this. So, the company needs a lot of improvement with regard to its promotional activities particularly with regard to the promotional plan.

The findings of this work also suggested that the company has different predetermined objectives on promotion which are broadly grouped as sales and company image. The company's promotional activities aimed at attracting new and keep existing customers to increase sales so as to maintain or improve market share. The company also needs its customers to have good feelings and positive image regarding its name that leads to improve company image and creates favorable climate for future sales. Further, the company conducted promotional activities with the hope of informing and educating its market about its activity. Finally, all these were hoping to generate competitive advantage against competitors. Generally, the company's promotional objectives were closely related to sales and communication or building and enhancing company image objectives. They are long-term, and stated in general terms; as a result it became extremely difficult for the company to determine what was accomplished by its promotional activities as well as to devise appropriate budget and promotional mix.

The company established budget through team-based decision. The company's method of budget determination did not consider the existing market demands in determining the promotion budget. The company's budgeting process also did not try to relate promotional expenditures or costs to the objectives that were intended to accomplish. This implies that the company did not consider marketing promotional activity as investment in which that required careful analysis and appropriate fund and its immediate impact on sales volume. Whatever competitors allocate and spend on promotional activities, and the company's sales increases or decreases were not considered by the company in establishing budget for its promotional activities. Moreover, the company spends insignificant amount on promotional activities compare to other activities of the company. Generally, the company established budget for promotional activities following affordable method.

The company used and considered advertisement, sales promotion, public relations, personal selling, and direct marketing as good promotional mix alternatives. But currently, the company undertakes its promotional activities through advertisement and sales promotion to some extent public relations, personal selling as of the responses of the respondents. To promote its products and in disseminating information among the potential and existing customers in order to draw and keep their attention: the company undertook advertisement. Advertisement helped the company to create awareness and relatively easy for the company to reach large audiences. To assess potential market and obtain promises from participants, the company used sales promotion activity which was currently dominated by exhibitions and trade fairs. To enhance relationship with its customers the company used personal selling and the company needs to look and give emphasis to this promotional mix as its products are technically complex, expensive and risky products. Direct marketing was the promotional mix that the company remains a lot to use it as promotional mix. It is the contemporary promotional mix in which the company can have relatively greater control.

The company make choice among these various alternative promotional mixes depending on market size and concentration, budget, number of people exposed to the mix, its relevance to engineering issues or its products, which were the most influential factors and customers' information need which was the least influential factor according to the response. Generally, the promotional activity of the company was dominated by advertisement, closely followed by sales promotion: undertaken through TV, radio, printed advertising materials and participating in exhibitions and trade fairs. Finally, direct marketing was the least practiced promotional mix by the company.

There are many problems that affect the company's promotional activities. The company, particularly the team members wrongly believed that in industrial goods like MIE's product, promotional activities produced insignificant results. As a result, the budget allocated for promotion was any amount that the company can afford. There was a serious problem in deciding budget for promotion in the company. The company gave less attention for promotional activities. Due to less emphasis given for promotion the company did not hired and assigned enough number of professionals and conduct promotional impact assessment. The company's products are technical, expensive as well as risky products; as a result it demands more personal selling promotional mix. But, the company used personal selling promotional mix in its improper way, i.e. as additional work undertaken by its sales officers. Together the above mentioned problems influenced the effectiveness of the company's promotional activities. Generally; budgeting, absence of promotional impact assessment, lack of personnel, and lack of awareness towards the role of promotion in the company or for the company's product were among the major problems of the company in relation to promotional activities.

5.3 Recommendations

Based on the findings of the study and the researcher's experience, the following suggestions can be put forwarded for the managerial implication to improve the promotional activities of the company and take the advantages of this twenty-first-century of manufacturing industry.

☞ Target audiences are the final receivers and users of the promotional activities and messages, as well as the base to devise promotional mix. And identification of target audiences is also one among the various components of promotional plan. But, the promotional plan of the company lacks effective target group identification. So, the company should conduct effective marketing research to identify target audiences' media habit, access, information need etc.

☞ The researcher feels that a promotional plan does not need to be rigid. It can and should allow for flexibility and creative efforts. By utilizing a promotional plan as a guide, basic operational activities can be understood and adapted more readily. Thus, after preparing effective promotional plan, the company should also review and up-grade it.

☞ The company should give emphasis to promotional activities by establishing a team to prepare, follow, monitor and up-date the promotional strategy.

☞ Most of the company's target audiences are business customers that are familiar and have access to e-commerce activities and facilities. As a result, using and keeping updated internet advertising, online showroom will have unreserved benefits for the company.

☞ The company produces technical, expensive and risky products that customers require with more and detailed information as well as face-to-face communication that help them to evaluate the purchase, so the company should give more emphasis to its personal selling –even by using selling teams rather than just one individual by recruiting and assigning qualified sales persons.

☞ To compete successfully in to day's globalization and competitive environment, promotion plays a vital role in performing different tasks. To do so, the company needs to have enough professionals and effective promotional measurement program that requires sufficient fund allocated scientifically. But the method that followed currently by the company for this purpose ignores the tasks to be implemented by promotion. Therefore, rather than allocating any arbitrary amount for promotion: tasks to be performed should be evaluated and the costs associated with each task should also be analyzed to establish budget for marketing promotion. More specifically, objective-task method should be followed to establish budget for promotional activities of the company.

☞ Measuring the results of promotion is vital to undertake adjustments and corrective actions. Therefore the company should measure the results of promotion effectively by developing promotional impact assessment program either by conducting research or looking into its sales. And it should be incorporated in its promotional plan.

5.4 Directions for Further Work

This work was designed out to assess the promotional activities of MIE P.L.C. But, due to time, financial and other restrictions there remain further to conduct the study as the replication of the present study. More specifically the following are the potential areas for this study;

The scope of the work have been limited only to MIE PLC, conducting further study by looking other similar manufacturing industries will be needed. The study assesses the promotional activities of MIE by looking only from company perspective, assessing the company's promotional activities from customers' perspective need to be further investigation. Exploring the benefits and impacts of promotional activities for the company remains further scope to conduct the study as the replication of this study. Evaluation the effectiveness of marketing promotional activities of the company also needs to be further investigation.

BIBLIOGRAPHY

Articles

- Balsko, Vincent J. and Charles H. Patti,(1984). "The advertising budgeting practices of industrial marketers", Journal of marketing 48(Fall), 104-110

- Churchill, Jr., GilbertA. (1985). "The determinants of salesperson performance; A Meta analysis", Journal of marketingresearch,22(May), 103-118

- David Stewart, (1996). "Allocating the promotional budget", Journal of Marketing Intelligence & Planning;; Vol. 14, No. 4 pp.34-38

- Dominique M. Hanssens and Barton A. Weitz, (1980). "The Effectiveness of Industrial Print Advertisements across Product Categories" , Journal of Marketing Research, Vol. 17, No. 3 pp. 294-306

- Donald W. Jackson, Jr.,Janet E. Keith and Richard K. Burdick, (1987). "The Relative Importance of Various Promotional Elements in Different Industrial Purchase Situations", Journal of Advertising, Vol.16,No.4 p25-33

- EEA, Ethiopian Economic Association, (2003/04). "Industrialization and Industrial policy in Ethiopia", Report on Ethiopian Economy, Vol. III, Addis Ababa, Ethiopia.

- Fotini Patsioura; Maro Vlachopoulou; Vicky Manthou, (2009). "A new advertising effectiveness model for corporate advertising web sites"; An International Journal, Vol. 16, No. 3, pp.372-386

- Gary L. Lilien, (Feb., 1979). "Modeling the Marketing Mix Decision for Industrial Products", Vol. 25, No. 2 pp. 191-204

- Jennifer Rowley, (1998). "Promotion and Marketing communications"; Vol. 47, No.8, p383-387

- Karl Hellman, Resultrek,(2005). "Strategy-driven B2B promotions", Journal of Business & Industrial Marketing, Volume: 20, Number: 1, pp: 4-11

- Kerin, Roger A. and William, (1987). "Assessing trade show functions and performance"; an exploratory study, Journal of marketing, 51(July), , 87-94

- Kristofer Ejebro, (2007). "Integrated marketing communications", Llea University of Technology

- Mesfin Berhane, (2007). "Model Development of Supply Chain Management System": A Case Study on Mesfin Industrial Engineering PLC. Addis Ababa, Ethiopia.
- M. Pilar López Belbeze; Joan Llonch Andreu; Rossano Eusebio, (2006). "Measures of marketing performance", International Journal of Contemporary Hospitality Management, Vol. 18, No. 2 pp.145 155
- Philip J. Kitchen, (1996). "Marketing communications; Promotional mix; Public relations"; Vol. 14, No.2 Pp. 5-12
- Rajasekhara Mouly Potluri, (2008). "Assessment of effectiveness of marketing communication mix elements in Ethiopian service sector", African Journal of Business Management Vol.2 (3), pp. 059-064, March
- Secil Tuncalp, (1999). "Evaluation of information sources in industrial marketing", Journal of Business & Industrial Marketing Vol.4 No.1(1999), pp.49-60
- Srinath Gopalakrishna and Gary L. Lilien, (1995). "A Three-Stage Model of Industrial Trade Show Performance", Marketing Science, Vol.14, No. 1 p. 22-42
- Urgaia Rissa Worku, (2007). "The growth of industrial manufacturing in Ethiopia and its contribution to GDP", Addis Ababa, Ethiopian.
- Weitz, (1981). "Effectiveness in sales interactions"; a contingency framework, journal of marketing, Vol. 45, p.85

Books
- Churchill (2003) sales force management 7th edition, Boston Mc-Grawhill Higher education
- Churchill, Gilbert A. and Dawn Iacobucci (2005), Marketing Research: Methodological Foundations 9th edition, Mason, Ohio: South-Western.
- E.Boone and L. Kurtz (1998), contemporary marketing 9th edition, Harcout Brace PLC.
- George E. Belch, Michael A. Belch (1993), introduction to advertising and promotion , 2nd edition, IRWIN, Australia
- Jakir Hossain(2006), The Use of Promotional Activities in the Tourism Industry: The Case of Bangladesh,
- James F. Engel; Martin R. Warshaw; Thomas C. Kinner, (1991), Promotional strategy, 7th edition, IRWIN
- *J.paul peter James H.Donnel, Jr. (198).) marketing management knowledge and skills,* IRWIN

- Michael D. Hutt; Thomas W.Speh (1995), business marketing management, 5th edition, Dryden press

- Michael J. Baker(1996), marketing an introductory text,6th edition, MacMillan

- Philip Kotler, (2000), Marketing Management, (Millennium Edition). New Jersey. Prentice- Hall.

- Philip Kottler (2004), Marketing management,9th edition, Prentice Hall

- Philip Kotler; Armstrong, Gary; Saunders, John; and Wong, Veronica (1999), *Principles of Marketing,* Prentice Hall Europe

- Philip Kotler, Kelvin Lane Keller, (2006), Marketing Management, 12th edition, Printice-Hal, New Delhi

- Philip Kotler; Wong, Veronica; Saunders, John; and Armstrong, Gary (2005) *Principles of Marketing*, 4th European Edition

- Ronald B.Marks(1988), personalselling,3rd edition, United States

- Stevens R.E, Loudon D.L, Clow K.E, (2003), Concise Encyclopedia of Professional Marketing

- Thomas J.R, Nelson J.K, Silverman S.J, (2005), Research methods in physical activity, 5th Edition

- Mesfin Industrial Engineering Company Profile, 2007

- Mesfin Industrial Engineering Company News Letters different volumes

Internet

- Carter McNamara, Basic Definitions, retrieved on 2009/11/23 from Webpage
  http://tutor2u.net/business/marketing/promotion/

- Carter McNamara, retrieved on 2009/11/20 from Webpage
  http://managementhelp.org/ad_prmot/defntion.htm

- John Halasz, promotional marketing strategies, retrieved on 2009/12/01 from Webpage
  http://ezinearticles.com/?Promotional-Marketing-Strategies&id=2209726

- Laura-Lake, 7 Steps to Planning a Productive and Successful Promotional Campaign, retrieved on
  2009/11/25 from Webpage http://develop a promotional campaign target marketing

- Linda Ann Nickerson; Paul Ashby; Atlaf Sahibzada, How to measure and evaluate the
  effectiveness of your advertising, retrieved on 2009/12/02 from Webpage
  http://www.helium.com/items/322648-how-to-measure-and-evaluate-the-effectiveness-of-your-advertising

- PRWeb, Tips for Press Release, retrieved on 2009/12/02 from Webpage
  http://www.prwebdirect.com/pressreleasetips.php

- *Rupal Jain,* Promotional Practices in Business http://en.wikipedia.org/wiki/Marketing/ retrieved
  2009/11/16

- Methodology retrieved on 2009/ 10/18 from Webpage http://www.answers.com/topic/methodology

- Marketing research retrieved 2009/10/20 from Webpage
  http://www.quickmba.com/marketing/research

- How to Write an Effective Press Release retrieved on 2009/ 12/01 from Webpage
  http://www.avenuewebmedia.com/how-write-effective-press-release

APPENDICES

Appendix-1: Interview Guide

MEKELLE UNIVERSITY
COLLEGE OF BUSINESS AND ECONOMICS
DEPARTMENT OF MANAGEMENT
GRADUATE PROGRAM IN MBA

Structured Interview Questionnaires

For a research entitled **'Assessment of Promotional Activities: A Case
Study in Mesfin industrial engineering, MIE PLC'**

Prepared by: Yemane Gidey

Under the super vision of

Principal advisor: Dr. Yassin Ibrahim (PhD)
Co-advisor: Gebrehiwot G/mariam (MPA)

Dec, 2009
Mekelle, Tigrai Ethiopia

Interview Guide

Interview date _____

Interview time _____

To be filled by Sales and Promotions Department

General questions
➢ What are the company's objectives to promote the product?

➢ What are the problems associated with promotion?

   ➢ Opinions about benefits of marketing promotion

Detailed questions
1. How much is the company's market share _____

2. Who are your local competitors? Please list down your major competitors

     a. _____
     b. _____
     c. _____
     d. _____

3. Do marketing promotions affect company's market share and position in the market?

   Why/ why not

4. Do marketing promotions affect the company's sales?

   Why/ why not

5. Do marketing promotions affect the climate for your future sales

   Why/ why not

6. Do marketing promotions help the company to compete in the market?

   Why/ why not

   Experience

7. Do marketing promotions help the company to inform and educate the market?

   Why/ why not

8. Current expenditure on marketing promotion is enough?

   Why/ why not

9. Promotional activity of the company is effective?

   Why/ why not

10. Are you using marketing promotions to create higher brand awareness, increased sales, or to enhance company image?

11. Do you think that your promotional activity will have social, economic, and business benefits?

12. Do you prefer to promote the product or company name?

13. How the company establishes budget for promotion?

14. When do you use promotional activity?(when introducing new product, regularly, occasionally)

15. Which promotional mix does the company use?(choose one or more of the following; Personal selling, Advertising, Sales promotion, Public relations, Direct marketing , Others)

16. Which factor/s influences your choice? Choose one or more factor from most influential to least; budget, customer needs, and market size and concentration, others)

17. Which advertisement tools/ medias does the company use?(choose one or more of the following; TV, Radio, printed materials, Internet, Direct mail, Others)

18.   Will promotional impact assessment is essential for the company?

19. Would you please mention the weaknesses of promotional activity undertaken by your company?(mentioned from the strongest to the weakest one)

20. What problems do you face with promotional activities of the company?

Other questions

Please forward your opinion on the promotional activity of the company

Interview Guide

Interview date _____

Interview time _____

To be filled by Public Relations Department

- What are the company's objectives to promote the product?
- Opinions about promotional mix
- What factors influence the company's choice of promotional mix?

Detailed questions

1. Do marketing promotions help the company to compete in the market?
2. Are you using marketing promotions to create higher brand awareness, increased sales, or to enhance company image?
3. Do marketing promotions help the company to inform and convince the market?
4. Do you think that your promotional activity will have social, economic, and business benefits?
5. When do you use promotional activity?(when introducing new product, regularly, occasionally)
6. Current expenditure on marketing promotion is enough?
    Why/ why not
7. Promotional activity of the company is effective?
    Why/ why not
8. How do you develop promotional plan?
9. Does the company effectively identify target audiences in preparing promotional plan?
10. Have you conduct promotional impact assessment to measure its result?
11. Will promotional impact assessment is essential for the company?
12. Which promotional mix does the company use?(choose one or more of the following; Personal selling, Advertising, Sales promotion, Public relations, Direct marketing , Others)
13. Which factor/s influences your choice? Choose one or more factor from most influential to least; budget, customer needs, and market size and concentration, others)
14. Which advertisement tools/ medias does the company use?(choose one or more of the following; TV, Radio, printed materials, Internet, Direct mail, Others)
15. What are the reasons for the selected promotional tools?

62

16. What methods does the company use to set budgets for promotion?
    - Affordable
    - Objective and task method
    - Percentage of sales
    - Competitive parity
    - Others
17. Is the currently applied method of budgeting is important to you?
18. Which promotional mix is being currently applied with minimum cost?
19. Which promotional mix is the most costly for the company?
20. Would you please mention the weaknesses of promotional activity undertaken by your company? (Mentioned from the strongest to the weakest one).
21. What problems do you face with promotional messages of the company?

Other questions

Any thing to add about marketing promotion

Interview Guide

Interview date _____

Interview time _____

To be filled by Business Development Department

General questions

> ➤ Opinions about promotional plan of the company

Detailed questions
1. Promotional activity of the company is effective?

    Why/ why not

2. Current expenditure on marketing promotion is enough?

    Why/ why not

3. Do you think that your promotional activity will have social, economic, and business benefit?

4. Does the company have promotional plan?

5. How the company develops promotional plan?

6. Does the company effectively identify target audiences in preparing promotional plan?

7. Do you have promotional impact assessment?

8. How the company establishes budget for promotion?

9. Does the company allocate enough budgets to promotion?

10. Will promotional impact assessment is essential for the company?

11. Which promotional mix does the company use? ?(choose one or more of the following: Personal selling, Advertising, Sales promotion, Public relations, Direct marketing , Others)

12. Which advertisement tools/ medias does the company use?(choose one or more of the following; TV, Radio, printed materials, Internet, Direct mail, Others)

13. Are you using marketing promotions to create higher brand awareness, increased sales, or to enhance company image?

14. Would please mention the weaknesses of promotional activity undertaken by your company? (Mentioned from the strongest to the weakest one)

15. What problems do you face while developing promotional plan of the company?

Other questions

Please forward your opinion on the promotional plan of the company

Interview Guide

Interview date _____

Interview time _____

To be filled by Finance Department

General questions

- ➢ How the company develops promotional budget?
- ➢ How much the company spends on promotional activity
- ➢ Opinions about promotional activity

Detailed questions

1. How much the budget of your sales is used for promotion?
2. Current expenditure on marketing promotion is enough?

    Why/ why not

3. Do you think that your promotional activity will have social, economic, and business benefits?
4. What methods does the company use to set budgets for promotion?
    - Affordable
    - Objective and task method
    - Percentage of sales
    - Competitive-parity method
    - Others
5. Is the currently applied method of budgeting is important to you?
6. Which promotional mix does the company use?(choose one or more of the following; Personal selling, Advertising, Sales promotion, Public relations, Direct marketing , Others)
7. Which advertisement tools/ medias does the company use?(choose one or more of the following; TV, Radio, printed materials, Internet, Direct mail, Others)
8. When do you promote?
9. Which promotional mix is being currently applied with minimum cost?
10. Which promotional mix is the most costly for the company?
11. Are you using marketing promotions to create higher brand awareness, increased sales, or to enhance company image?

12. Promotional activity of the company is effective?

    Why/ why not

13. Will promotional impact assessment is essential for the company?

14. Would you please mention the weaknesses of promotional activity undertaken by your company? (Mentioned from the strongest to the weakest one).

15. What problems do you face with promotional activities?

Other questions

Please forward your opinion on the promotional plan of the company

Appendix-2: Promotional Plan of MIE

2.1 One year Promotional Plan-2008

S. No	Tasks to implemented	Budget	Time specification
1	TV advertisement	40,000	Dec19, Jan8, Mar 2&20, May28
2	News paper advertisement	40,000	from Nov-June
3	Quarterly News Letter	45,000	Dec, Mar, Jul
4	Gift materials(give away items	50,000	Dec and Jan
5	Exhibitions and trade fairs	50,000	Feb21-27, April 10-13, May06-08, May15-19 2008
6	Stickers	5000	Dec
7	Promotional film and photos	50,000	from Nov-June
8	Bill board	3,000	Dec
9	Website	20,000	Dec

2.2 One year Partial Operational Plan of PR- Department-for 2010

S. No	Objectives	Strategy	Major activities	Time frame				Budget
				1st quarter	2nd quarter	3rd quarter	4th quarter	
1	Publicizing updated information about the company	Updating the existing company profile and brochure	Designing	■				150,000
			Publishing	■				
		News letter production	Publishing	■	■	■	■	120,000
			distribution	■	■	■	■	
		Website administration	Production of news and profile	■	■	■	■	–
			Administration	■	■	■	■	
2	Promoting the company	TV advertisement	Advertising	■	■	■	■	184,000
		Participating in exhibition	Preparation of exhibition materials	■	■		■	150,000
			displaying		■	■	■	
		News paper and magazine advertisement	Preparation of advertisement design	■	■	■	■	104,000
			Advertising	■	■	■	■	
		Radio advertisement	Production	■		■	■	40,000
			Advertising	■	■	■	■	
		Preparation and distribution of gift articles	Preparation	■	■	■	■	50,000
			Distribution		■	■	■	
		Bill board erection	Design works	■				30,000
			Erection	■				

68

Appendix-3 MIE's Various Actual Cost Structure for Selected Five Years

MIE's Total Promotional Expenditure of Selected Five Years

Year	Promotional expenditure	
	Budgeted	Actual
2004	504,000	306,993
2005	200,000	97,379
2006	300,000	76,151
2007	160,000	94,183
2008	160,000	275,785

MIE's Partial Income Statement

Year	Sales	Cost of goods sold	Operating expense	Selling and distribution expenses	Promotional expenses
2004	73,842,715	64,589,036	7,501,301	2,608,668	306,993
2005	49,755,736	43,534,229	29,802,468	639,024	97,379
2006	153,587,067	109,805,707	9,775,788	622,016	76,151
2007	197,855,859	150,281,926	11,902,851	1,365,391	94,183
2008	167,761,775	134,906,543	13,843,483	1,278,518	275,785

Appendix-4 Partial view of Mesfin Industrial Engineering

Appendix -5 Organizational Structure of MIE

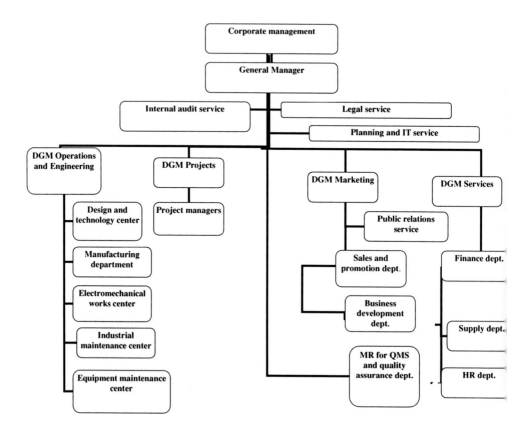

Lightning Source UK Ltd.
Milton Keynes UK
UKOW050808300911

179551UK00001B/161/P